Kit Carson's Autobiography

Yours
C Carson—

Kit Carson's Autobiography

EDITED BY

MILO MILTON QUAIFE

UNIVERSITY OF NEBRASKA
PRESS

Lincoln/London

The Bison Book edition of *Kit Carson's Autobiography* appeared as No. 33 in the Lakeside Classics, published in 1935, and is reprinted by arrangement with the Lakeside Press, R. R. Donnelley & Sons Co., Chicago, who are the sole proprietors of its special contents.

International Standard Book Number 0–8032–5031–2

Library of Congress Catalog Number 66–4130

First Bison Book printing March, 1966

Most recent printing shown by first digit below:

10

⊗

Manufactured in the United States of America

Contents

Historical Introduction

ments arrived, ~~then we disposed~~ and traded of our Beaver to the
traders that came up with our equipment. We ~~remained~~ in our
in Summer quarters till September. ~~&c~~

~~There was in~~ the party of ~~captain Drips~~, a large Frenchman one of those ~~overbearing~~ kind ~~and very strong~~ he
made a practice of whipping every ~~man~~ ~~that~~ he was
displeased with and that was nearly ~~all~~. One day
after he had beaten two or three men, he said ~~that~~ for the
Frenchmen he had no trouble ~~to flog~~ and as for the A-
mericans he would ~~take~~ a switch and switch them
I did not like such talk from any man, so I told him
that ~~I was the best American~~ ~~I could~~ ~~peacefully disposed~~ ~~like~~ many
trash him ~~only on account of being afraid~~ sound ~~and that,~~ and
if he made use of any more of such expressions, ~~I he~~
would ~~cut his guns~~, he said nothing, but started for
his rifle, mounted his horse and made his appea-
rence in front of the camp. As soon as I saw ~~him~~ that he was
I mounted my horse also took the first ~~weapon~~
I could get ahold of which was a pistol. Gallopped
up to him and demanded if I was the one ~~intended~~
he intended to shoot, our horses heads touching he
~~said~~ no but at the same time drawing back his
gun so he could ~~get~~ a better shot, I was ~~free as~~
pared and allowed him to ~~draw~~ his gun, We both
fired at the same time, all present said but one
report was heard, I shot him through the arm
and his ball ~~skipped~~ my head, cutting my hair and
~~the powder~~ covering my eye, the muzzle of his gun
being near my ~~head~~ when he fired. During our
stay in camp we had no more bother with this bully.
~~Frenchman~~ On the first of September we departed on
our fall hunt trapping the yellow Stone & Big horn
rivers, and then crossed over to the three forks of the Missouri

Historical Introduction

M ANY volumes of *The Lakeside Classics* Series have been devoted to narratives of trade and exploration in the trans-Mississippi West. If we include under this designation the Canadian Northwest, with the single exception of Mrs. Kinzie's *Wau Bun*, from 1923 to the present time every issue has been devoted to this area. All of the volumes thus published have been reprints of earlier, and now rare or obscure books, and the reader who has preserved a complete set of *The Lakeside Classics* possesses a rather extensive library of the more important sources for the development of the American West.

In the world of the silver screen cycles come and go, but one type of picture, the "western," flourishes perennially. Therein the observer can detect a great truth of American history. The mastery of the frontier is the great romance of America, and its story engages the deepest affections of our people. In this story two popular heroes stand preëminent, Daniel Boone and Kit Carson. Other men may have been no less brave, and no less skilled in wilderness lore, but the popular fame of Boone and Carson as the outstanding frontier heroes of their respective generations is securely established.

Seldom, however, has a hero entered less auspiciously upon the pathway to fame and glory than Carson. Reared on the crude Missouri frontier, physically small and unimpressive, wholly without formal education, orphaned in childhood, and apprenticed to the prosaic craft of a leather worker, he began his western career by running away from his home and employer. The latter advertised the fact to the world by inserting this notice in the *Missouri Intelligencer:*

Notice is hereby given to all persons,

That Christopher Carson, a boy about 16 years old, small of his age, but thick-set; light hair, ran away from the subscriber, living in Franklin, Howard County, Missouri, to whom he had been bound to learn the saddler's trade, on or about the first of September last. He is supposed to have made his way to the upper part of the state. All persons are notified not to harbor, support, or assist said boy under the penalty of the law. One cent reward will be given to any person who will bring back the said boy.

Franklin, Oct. 6, 1826.   DAVID WORKMAN

Neither the "penalty of the law," nor the inducement of one cent reward, however,

deterred Charles Bent—if, indeed, he ever
saw the advertisement—noted merchant of
the Santa Fé Trail, from "harboring" the
tow-headed boy who thus made his first appearance upon the literary horizon; and in
the humble rôle of "cavvy" boy in Bent's
Santa Fé caravan, in the autumn of 1826,
sixteen-year old Kit Carson embarked upon
his notable career. Thirty years later, a post-
graduate of the University of the Wilderness,
and for a decade past a national hero, Carson was persuaded to appease the popular
appetite for information about his career by
dictating to a literate friend his own story of
his life to date. Less than thirty thousand
words in all, and characterized by a modesty
which oftentimes tends to mislead through
understatement, the simple autobiography
thus produced became the basis of all subsequent lives of Carson. Yet until 1926 it remained unprinted, and until the present
moment even the biographers of Carson have
been ignorant of the circumstances under
which it was produced. How, and why,
these things came to pass, we shall endeavor
to unfold.

The proverb about a hero being without
honor in his own immediate neighborhood
has no application to Carson. His fame was
first established among his own mountain

men, years before the outside world ever
heard of him, and until the day of his death
his neighbors, red and white, friendly and
hostile, yielded ungrudging tribute to his remarkable qualities of character and leadership.

When, quite by chance, he encountered
John C. Frémont in 1842 and diffidently
offered to become his guide, he was so wholly
unknown to the public that Frémont had to
take time to investigate his references before
venturing to engage him. The two men became firm friends, and each has expressed in
unstinted terms his admiration for the other.
Both men profited by the association, for if
Frémont's success as "Pathfinder" of the
Rockies was largely due to Carson's skill and
guidance, Carson's introduction to the world
outside the mountains was wholly owing to
Frémont. That popular hero possessed journalistic talent of a high order, and his labors
to acquaint the world with his achievements
were ably seconded by his talented wife and
his famous father-in-law, Senator Benton.
Frémont suddenly dawned upon the public
mind of the early forties, a veritable earth-
bound Lindbergh, and Kit Carson was his
fidus Achates. On the floor of the United
States Senate, in the public press, by word-
of-mouth report and rumor, Carson's deeds

were related and magnified. The paper-backs took him up, and before long a wholly imaginary superman had taken shape in the public mind, while the real hero, still in the prime of life and with half his career yet before him, was pursuing his unostentatious course of life in the remote American Southwest.

The popular interest in Carson's career was evidently discussed among his friends, and by them was discussed with him, and at length he entered upon the unwonted task of dictating his story. When it was finished, he signed with a legible hand (the extent, apparently, of his mastery of penmanship) his name to the concluding paragraph: "The foregoing I hereby transfer to Mr. Jesse B. Turly to be used as he may deem proper for our joint benefit." The significance of this statement seems to have escaped his biographers heretofore, who to the extent that they have utilized the autobiography at all, have ascribed its production to his authorized biographer, Dr. De Witt C. Peters. The present Editor began his work imbued with the same idea, but in the course of his efforts to unravel the facts attendant upon the history of the autobiography, was compelled to abandon it.

To this history the attention of the reader may now be invited. Dr. Peters was an army surgeon who served in the Southwest for a time in the fifties[1] and there made the acquaintance of Carson. In 1858 he published at New York *The Life and Adventures of Kit Carson, the Nestor of the Rocky Mountains, from Facts Narrated by Himself,* an octavo volume of 534 pages. The "facts" were, of course, taken from Carson's manuscript autobiography, which Peters, or his literary helper, expanded to five times the modest dimensions of the original. Carson formally certified that Peters was his only authorized biographer, and the accuracy of the recital was attested by three of his old-time Taos friends.

The vicissitudes of the manuscript autobiography provide an interesting and suggestive story. Dr. Peters left the army in the autumn of 1856 for an extended sojourn in Europe. Subsequent to his return, he married, and two sons, William Theodore and Clinton Peters were born. William became a poet, and resided in Paris, where he died in utmost destitution in 1905. Clinton became

---

[1] He was commissioned, August 15, 1854, and left the army October 1, 1856. These dates fix the extreme limits of his personal intercourse with Carson prior to the publication of the biography. He was again stationed in New Mexico for several years beginning in the summer of 1867, and may have been in contact with Carson during the last few months of his life.

an artist, and lived in New York City. Following the death of William, Clinton went to Paris to take charge of his effects. After completing, as he thought, a survey of them, he discovered an old trunk in the basement of a house whose owner informed him that the trunk belonged to Peters. Its contents proved to be "chiefly old receipted bills and various bundles of unimportant papers" and Peters was about to leave the place and order the papers to be destroyed, when his eye was arrested by the words "Kit Carson" on the cover of one of the packages.

Examination proved it to be the autobiography, of whose existence Clinton Peters had hitherto known nothing. He carried the manuscript back to New York, where he presently engaged a public stenographer to make two typed copies of it. In 1909, the centennial of Carson's birth, he endeavored to sell one of the copies for magazine publication, but after several rejections, he abandoned the effort, and soon after (1909 or 1910) disposed of the original manuscript, one of the typed copies, and Dr. Peters' own annotated copy of the Life of Carson to Joseph Thevett Pike of New York. The latter (through the agency of the Lexington Book Store) soon sold the manuscript for a small sum to Arthur H. Clark of Cleveland, who also obtained without cost the typed copy and the annotated biography. From the latter the manuscript passed in the spring of 1911 to Edward E. Ayer, the noted Chicago collector, to find a permanent resting-place in the great collection of Americana presented by him to the Newberry Library.

In the autumn of 1921, Charles L. Camp of Berkeley, California, an active student of Carson's career, contacted Clinton Peters in New York, and in addition to obtaining from him his story of the manuscript autobiography, purchased his remaining typed copy of it. He subsequently purchased, from a book dealer, the other typed copy, which was being advertised as the original manuscript, and learning of the whereabouts of the latter (now in the Newberry Library) visited Chicago and corrected his two copies, by comparison with it. In 1922 he published somewhat extensive extracts from the autobiography in the first volume of the *California Historical Society Quarterly*, in an article entitled "Kit Carson in California," and two years later transferred one of his copies to Blanche C. Grant of Taos, who published it in 1926 as a paper-covered volume of 138 pages with the title, *Kit Carson's Own Story of His Life as Dictated to Col. and Mrs. D. C. Peters About 1856–57 And Never Before Published.*

Historical Introduction

The original autobiography is written in a clear, firm hand; at some subsequent date, some editor undertook to revise it, apparently with a view to publication, and the interlining and amendments are in places so numerous as to render it difficult to determine the original text. Clinton Peters in 1921 told Mr. Camp that the original penmanship was the handwriting of his mother, and that the autobiography had been dictated by Carson to Dr. Peters during his visits to the surgeon while the latter was stationed in New Mexico. These statements were too incautiously credited by Camp, who passed them on to Miss Grant. In her book they assume the form that the autobiography "is for the most part in the handwriting of Mrs. Peters, though at times the Colonel helped with the writing," which was done during Carson's frequent visits to the family, then stationed at "some fort near Taos."

That Clinton Peters had no real knowledge concerning the production of the autobiography, and that his account of it, as given to Mr. Camp, is wholly erroneous, is obvious. It might be presumed that he would speak with authority in the matter of his mother's handwriting, but even here he was one hundred per cent wrong. A comparison of her known handwriting with the manuscript autobiography clearly discloses that the latter was not penned by Mrs. Peters. If there were any room for doubting the correctness of this judgment (in the writer's mind there is none), it would be resolved by the further fact that at the time of Dr. Peters' first sojourn in the Southwest (1854–56), when the autobiography was written, *there was no Mrs. Peters* to collaborate in its production. Letters written by Dr. Peters from Paris to his sister in September, 1857, and in September, 1859, disclose that he was still a bachelor, and although yearning for matrimony had not yet found an object upon whom to fix his affections.[2] Although we have no information as to who the future Mrs. Peters was, or where

[2] Letters in possession of Mr. Camp. The place of writing the second letter (dated Sept. 28, 1859) is not indicated. In the 1873 and later editions of his life of Carson, Peters states that he remained in Europe four years (1856–60). Mr. Camp, in 1921, however, noted among the papers of Clinton Peters a certificate, dated June 1, 1860, indicating that Dr. Peters had been attached to the Northern Dispensary in New York City the "past two years," which points to the conclusion that he may have returned to America in 1858. This conclusion, if valid, aids in solving another troublesome point (to be noted *post*) with respect to Dr. Peters' agency in bringing out his life of Carson at New York in 1858.

Historical Introduction

Dr. Peters made her acquaintance, it is clear that she was not his wife and literary aide in New Mexico in the years from 1854 to 1856.

We may now consider Dr. Peters' own claim to a share in the production of the autobiography. It may readily be conceded that if he induced Carson to relate his life story to him, and if Dr. Peters dictated the narrative as it was written down, the question who performed the labor of writing it is relatively unimportant. It requires merely the reading of the preface which Dr. Peters supplied for his biography of Carson, however, to discover that he himself claimed *no credit for*, *nor any agency in*, the production of the autobiography; on the contrary, by clear implication, he expressly negatives such a claim. In common with "thousands," he relates, he had long desired to see Carson's biography in print, without flattering himself that to him would be "assigned" the task of producing it. Finally, "at the urgent solicitation of many personal friends," Carson had dictated the narrative, which was "then" put at Peters' disposal. Peters was a warm admirer of Carson, whose friendship he was proud to advertise, but he makes no claim to having had any agency in producing the autobiography, and both his own words and those of Carson himself indicate that he did not have any.[3]

A final, and conclusive piece of evidence on this point remains to be cited. Dr. Peters left New Mexico for Europe in 1856, his biography of Carson was published in 1858 and the two men did not see each other again until after the Civil War.[4] The first edition of the biography is prefaced by a formal certificate by Carson, dated at Taos, Nov. 3, 1858, that Peters is his only authorized biographer. The original manuscript of this certificate is fortunately preserved with the autobiography itself in the Newberry

[3] Contradicting the foregoing, after Carson's death in 1868, Peters wrote a letter about him for publication in the *Army and Navy Journal* in which he told of Carson's friendship for him and asserted that he "even dictated his life to me, which I endeavored to write," etc. Letter reprinted in Miss Grant's *Kit Carson's Own Story*, 136–37. The most charitable view to take of this assertion is that it was prompted by a failing memory. Dr. Peters made no such claim when writing the preface to his biography a dozen years earlier, when Carson was alive, his own memory fresh, and when he had a powerful motive for doing so, had the facts permitted; and both his own statements at that time and those of Carson (to be presently discussed) controvert it.

[4] On this point see Peters' statement in his biography of Carson, 1873 edition, pp. 549–50. The statement there made is supplemented by the official record of Dr. Peters' military service, which has been furnished the Editor by the War Department.

Library. The penmanship of the two (excepting Carson's signature) is identical. Since Dr. Peters was in Europe from 1856 to 1860,[5] and since he did not see Carson from the time of his departure until after the Civil War, he is not the man who wrote the autobiography in 1856, and who, still in touch with Carson, penned at Taos on Nov. 3, 1858, this certificate.

With the confusion concerning the supposed agency of Dr. Peters and his wife in producing the autobiography dispelled, we are at last free to consider what the real story was. We have seen that a full decade before the writing of the autobiography in 1856, Carson's name and fame had become familiar to the American public, and that a widespread desire to know the facts about his adventurous career had developed. Despite his fame, Carson never earned much money, and he was struggling to maintain a home and develop an estate for his still-growing family. Under these circumstances, it was entirely proper that he should yield to the urging of his friends to supply the public with the unwritten and largely unknown narrative of his adventures, and that he should anticipate obtaining some financial

[5] The evidence indicating that he may have been back in New York from 1858 to 1860 has been noted *ante*.

reward from his undertaking. Illiterate himself, he must invoke the aid of some literate friend to turn his recital into presentable English and to find a literary market for it. The relation of one's life-story is a task of considerable magnitude, particularly for an unschooled man whose life has been spent in such an environment as Carson's had. Many sessions must be devoted to the task, and the literary assistant would naturally be selected from among Carson's Taos friends and neighbors. Internal evidence discloses that the autobiography was completed in the autumn of 1856. Its final sentence, beneath which Carson subscribed his signature, reads: "The foregoing I hereby transfer to Mr. Jesse B. Turly to be used as he may deem proper for our joint benefit." Herein is the confirmation, from Carson himself, of the conclusion already derived from Dr. Peters' statements, that the latter had nothing to do with the preparation of the autobiography; for it is unthinkable that if Dr. Peters had inspired it, and had himself been Carson's assistant in producing it, this sentence could have been written. Obviously Carson regarded himself and Jesse B. Turly as joint owners of the manuscript, and the latter as his literary agent in the business of finding a market for it. Dr. Peters, who departed for

Historical Introduction

Europe just at the time the manuscript was being completed may have known that it was· being prepared, but he clearly had at this time no proprietary interest in it.

The facts attending the authorship and publication of Dr. Peters' biography, based upon the Carson manuscript, demand our further attention. The Library of Congress is authority for the statement that the book was first published at New York by W. R. C. Clark and Co. in 1858, and the copyright notice of the book bears this date. Carson's certificate that Peters was his authorized biographer (dated at Taos, Nov. 3, 1858), however, indicates that the book could not have been published before the closing weeks of the year, and the first copy in the Detroit Public Library (which the Editor has used) gives 1859 as the year of publication. Whether the precise date be late in 1858 or early in 1859 is immaterial to our immediate problem, which is, how could Peters, pursuing his medical studies in Europe from 1856 to 1860, have gotten control of the autobiography and have performed the task of turning it into a 534-page octavo volume? If he actually came back to New York in 1858, and was attached to the Northern Dispensary there during the two ensuing years, the difficulties of authorship, as also of maintain-

ing contact with the Taos literary firm of
Carson and Turly, become materially les-
sened. In either event, it is established that
Peters had no personal contact with Carson
after leaving New Mexico in the autumn of
1856. Agent Turly must have continued his
efforts to market the autobiography, until
he effected the arrangement with Peters
(either in Paris or in New York) which even-
tuated in the publication of the biography
by the latter late in 1858 or early in 1859.
It proved a fortunate enterprise for Peters,
for if Clinton Peters' statement to Mr. Camp
in 1921 is accurate, he realized a profit of
about $20,000 from it—no mean fortune for
a young army surgeon, still engaged upon his
medical studies.

Although Dr. Peters assumes the responsibility of authorship of the book, he credits
his friend C. Hatch Smith of Brooklyn with
rendering "valuable assistance in revising,
correcting and arranging his manuscript."
This fact would call for no comment, did it
not invite the question of precisely how extensive the contribution of C. Hatch Smith
to the resultant biography was. By the ex-
ercise of arts familiar to all literary workers,
Peters' biography expanded to five-fold dimensions the simple manuscript of Carson.
How could Peters have carried on this work,

while pursuing his studies in Paris? If in New York from 1858 on, he was favorably situated to do it, provided the time needed for the work of authorship could be found in the midst of his medical work. Obviously he sought the literary aid of Smith, and the question may be asked (though we have no means of answering it) whether Smith's responsibility for the biography is not greater (and Dr. Peters' correspondingly smaller) than has commonly been supposed. Certain of its rather conspicuous qualities moved Stanley Vestal, recent biographer of Carson, to characterize Peters as an "ass." Although not a seasoned westerner, his two-year sojourn in the Southwest must have given him some real measure of understanding of mountain men and frontier conditions, and it seems possible that Vestal's impatient shaft has been launched at the wrong individual.

Who, then, did assist Carson in his difficult task of producing his autobiography? We can, at present, only offer a guess, which some future investigator, less pressed for time than the present Editor, and more fortunately situated with respect to access to local sources of information, is invited to follow up. There were Turlys, or Turleys, in Taos and vicinity from a comparatively early date in the American invasion of the

Historical Introduction

Southwest. One member of the family established Turley's mill, a few miles from Taos, where the battle connected with the native uprising against the Americans early in 1847 occurred. Twitchell, the historian of New Mexico, states (*Old Santa Fé*, 289-91) that these Turleys came from the vicinity of Old Franklin, Mo., long prior to the Mexican War. This was the vicinity where Carson grew up, and from which he ran away to New Mexico in 1826. Turning to the *History of Howard and Cooper Counties, Missouri*, published in 1883, we find numerous traces of the Turly (Turley) clan as pioneers and as descendants of pioneers in that region. In particular, we find (pp. 997-98) a sketch of Jesse B. Turley, native of Madison County, Ky. (Kit Carson's natal county), born about the year 1800, who settled as a young man in Cooper County, Missouri. He engaged in the Santa Fé trade and "year after year for a generation" made his trips across the plains "as regularly as the seasons come and go." He made a comfortable fortune in the business, which he continued until stricken down by death at Santa Fé in August, 1861. Such a man could not have been a stranger to Carson, and it is not improbable that Turley, the older man, was familiar with Carson from his boyhood on.

Historical Introduction

With his Missouri connections, and his established business ability, he would have been as suitable an agent to market Carson's narrative as anyone available to him; and the suggestion is hazarded that it was he who labored with Carson to produce it, and that his was the pen that wrote it down.

In the process of editing the manuscript for publication, certain problems were encountered whose solution by the Editor must now be explained. It is, of course, an established principle of historical scholarship that in the printing of documents the original copy be truthfully reproduced; if any divergence from the original be undertaken, the editor must apprise the reader of this fact, and indicate to him the nature of the change, or changes, made. In dealing with the Carson manuscript, we face the fact that it does not record, and we do not know, what Carson actually said. Differently stated, we know that both language and orthography are the work of Carson's collaborator, who listened to his story and recorded it in words correctly spelled and in sentences frequently awkward, but at least measurably correctly composed. As for Carson, not only was he illiterate, but the language he employed differed markedly from ordinary literary English.[6] His collaborator made no effort to record the story verbatim as it fell from the lips of Carson; instead, he transposed it into reasonably orthodox English, correctly spelled, in the main. While there might be valid reasons for printing Carson's precise words, if we had them, the Editor has deemed it undesirable to reproduce the precise locutions of his aid and interpreter; and wholly logical to complete the process, begun by the latter, of transmuting the ideas expressed by Carson into simple, grammatical English. Our printing of the autobiography, therefore, aims to present as accurately as possible, in ordinary present-day English, the ideas and facts Carson intended to convey, but it makes no pretense of reproducing the manuscript verbatim.

[6] Many books reproduce more or less accurately the patois which Carson and other mountain men habitually employed. A sample (possibly exaggerated) of their everyday speech is afforded by George F. Ruxton's description of Bill Williams in his *Life in the Far West* (New York, 1849), Chap. V. Williams was reputed to have been a preacher in Missouri, which may imply that he had some slight formal education, while we know that Carson had none. For similar examples of the speech of Jim Bridger and Jim Baker, friends and contemporaries of Carson, see Col. R. B. Marcy, *Thirty Years of Army Life on the Border*. . . . (New York, 1866), 39–40 and 403–404.

Historical Introduction

Biographies of Carson are numerous,[7] and it is no part of our present task to trace his career in detail. A final caution to the reader, however, may be in order. Carson was so modest and undemonstrative, and the exploits of his everyday life were frequently so remarkable, that the reader must supplement his simple narration with the resources of his own imagination if he is to appreciate the true nature of the things Carson relates. We may point these remarks with a pertinent illustration. Carson describes in a single page his journey from Los Angeles to Taos in the spring of 1848. George D. Brewerton, an intelligent young army officer who accompanied Carson on this trip, devotes 150 pages to his account of it.[8] Carson disposes of the first half of the journey in a single sentence; Brewerton devotes over one hundred pages to this part of his story. Less than a paragraph suffices Carson to describe the hazardous crossing of Grand River; Brewerton's recital of the same feat fills seven

[7] Perhaps the most useful is Edwin L. Sabin's *Kit Carson Days* (Chicago, 1914). A revised edition, with several additional chapters (not seen by the present editor), was issued in 1935. Stanley Vestal's *Kit Carson, the Happy Warrior,* is a recent impressionistic biography which contains some new information.

[8] George Douglas Brewerton, *Overland With Kit Carson.* . . . (New York, 1930).

pages. Four sentences are utilized by Carson
in relating the encounter of his little band of
followers with "several hundred" Apache and
Utah Indians, whom with consummate craft
and determination he outwitted and over-
awed; Brewerton devotes six pages to the
story of this encounter. On this occasion, as
on uncounted others, the lives of the entire
party depended for their preservation on the
skill and wit of Carson alone; and in a situation which might well have appalled the most
courageous man, he moved as surely and—
later—talked about it as simply, as though
it were an ordinary routine operation, as
for Carson it probably was. Carson writes,
"They made demonstrations of hostility and
we retired into the brush, where we permitted only a few of them to approach us." The
wild scene which lay back of this simple
statement is depicted thus by Brewerton:
"We had scarcely made these hurried preparations before the whole horde were upon us,
and had surrounded our position. For the next
fifteen minutes a scene of confusion and excitement ensued which baffles my powers of
description. On the one hand the Indians
pressed closely in, yelling, aiming their spears,
and drawing their bows, while their chiefs,
conspicuous from their activity, dashed here
and there among the crowd, commanding

and directing their followers. On the other side, our little band, with the exception of those who had lost their rifles in Grand River, stood firmly around the caballada; Carson, a few paces in advance, giving orders to his men and haranguing the Indians. His whole demeanor was now so entirely changed that he looked like a different man; his eyes fairly flashed, and his rifle was grasped with all the energy of an iron will.

"'There,' cried he, addressing the savages, 'is our line, cross it if you dare, and we begin to shoot. You ask us to let you in, but you won't come unless you ride over us. You say you are friends, but you don't act like it. No, you don't deceive us so, we know you too well; so stand back, or your lives are in danger.'"

In moments of repose the singularly unassuming demeanor of Carson did little to advertise the qualities of resolute leadership which he displayed in times of crisis. To casual strangers he seemed wholly to belie the character their fancy had painted, so that stories are told of men asking to have Carson pointed out to them, and when this had been done, refusing to believe that it was actually the great trapper who stood before them. In the final analysis, Carson's principal asset was his character—gentle, generous, honest, and courageous—a veritable nineteenth-century Chevalier Bayard of the western wilderness. America does well to cherish his memory; fitter material for the making of heroes is seldom found.

It is a pleasure, in closing, to acknowledge publicly the kindness of George B. Utley, Librarian of the Newberry Library, for permission to utilize the Carson manuscript. Generous assistance has been accorded, also, by Mr. Charles L. Camp of the University of California, whose unique knowledge concerning the manuscript autobiography has been freely levied upon. To Dr. Floyd Shoemaker, Secretary of the State Historical Society of Missouri, Professor W. S. Campbell ("Stanley Vestal") of the University of Oklahoma, Dr. Le Roy R. Hafen, Curator of the State Historical Society of Colorado, and Professor Lansing B. Bloom of the University of New Mexico, the Editor is further indebted for response to his drafts upon the special knowledge which they command.

M. M. QUAIFE

Detroit Public Library,
June 1, 1935

Kit Carson's Autobiography

Kit Carson's
Autobiography

I WAS born on December 24, 1809, in Madison County, Kentucky. My parents[1] moved to Missouri when I was one year old and settled in what is now Howard County. For two or three years after our arrival we had to remain forted,[2] and it was necessary

[1] Lindsay Carson, born about 1755 and possibly a native of Scotland, grew up in North Carolina. He served as a soldier in the Revolution, and subsequent to the death of his first wife in 1793, migrated to Kentucky, where in 1797 he married Rebecca Robinson, a native of that state. According to the history of Howard County, Mo., they had eight children (ten according to *Dict. Am. Biog.*), four boys and four girls; Christopher, hero of our present narrative, was the third son of the family.

Lindsay Carson removed to the Boone's Lick country, settling in Franklin Township, Howard County, Mo., probably early in 1811. In 1818 he was killed by a falling limb, while engaged in burning timber. Four years later the widow married Joseph Martin.

[2] The Boone's Lick country was much harassed by the Indians during the War of 1812. The settlers "forted" for mutual protection, the forts being commonly log houses, loop-holed and barricaded. The Carson family lived near Fort Hempstead, and Lindsay and Moses Carson, father and brother of Kit, were enrolled among

to have men stationed at the ends of the fields for the protection of those that were laboring.

For fifteen years I lived in Missouri, and during that time I dwelt in Howard County. I was apprenticed to David Workman to learn the saddler's trade, and remained with him two years.[3] The business did not suit me and, having heard so many tales of life in the mountains of the West, I concluded to leave him. He was a good man, and I often recall the kind treatment I received at his hands. But taking into consideration that if I re-

its defenders. Illustrative of the conditions of the time, is the old-age story of a survivor, who lived in Fort Hempstead, that there were seven widows in the fort, and the penalty fixed by the settlers for falling asleep on sentry duty was to require the offender to grind a peck of corn for each widow.

[3] David Workman lived in Old Franklin, which flourished in the decade of the twenties as the westernmost outpost of settlement on the Missouri and the entrepôt for the trade with distant Santa Fé. An illuminating picture of the town in this period is given by Jonas Viles in "Old Franklin; a Frontier Town of the Twenties," in *Miss. Valley Hist. Rev.*, IX, 269–82. Since Carson was a minor, whose father was dead, he must have been apprenticed to Workman by his mother or his step-father. The boy terminated his service by the simple process of running away. His own explanation agrees substantially with Louis Houck's terse observation (*Hist. of Mo.*, III, 146) that the labor became "irksome" to him.

mained with him and served my apprenticeship, I would have to pass my life in labor
that was distasteful to me, and being anxious
to travel for the purpose of seeing different
countries, I concluded to join the first party
that started for the Rocky Mountains.

In August, 1826, I had the good fortune to
hear of one bound for that country. I made
application to join this party, and was accepted, without any difficulty. On the road,
one of the party, Andrew Broadus, met with
a serious accident. He was taking his rifle
out of a wagon for the purpose of shooting a
wolf and, in drawing it out, accidentally discharged it, receiving the contents in the
right arm. We had no medical man with us,
and he suffered greatly from the effects of
the wound. His arm began to mortify and
we all were aware that amputation was
necessary. One of the party stated that he
could do it.[4] Broadus was prepared for any

[4] Miss Grant states (*Kit Carson's Own Story of His
Life*, 10) that Carson himself was the volunteer who
performed the amputation, citing Peters' biography as
her authority. Peters, who spins out the recital of the
incident to about two pages, merely states that Carson
and two others performed the amputation. To the
present Editor it seems improbable that a band of
veteran plainsmen would have assigned the chief rôle
in such an emergency to their newest recruit, a tender-
foot, and still a mere boy. Carson knew how to be

experiment that was considered of service to him. The doctor set to work and cut the flesh with a razor and sawed the bone with an old saw. The arteries being cut, to stop the bleeding, he heated a kingbolt from one of the wagons and burned the affected parts, and then applied a plaster of tar taken off the wheel of a wagon. The patient became perfectly well before our arrival in New Mexico.

We arrived at Santa Fé in November, and I proceeded to Fernandez de Taos, my present place of residence, the same month, and remained during the winter with an old mountaineer by the name of Kincade. In the spring of 1827 I started for the States, but on the Arkansas River I met a party en route for New Mexico; I joined them and remained with them till their arrival in Santa Fé. I then hired with a man, whose name I have forgotten, to drive team, my wages being one dollar per day. I remained in his employ till our arrival at El Paso, when I took my discharge and returned to Santa Fé.

I left Santa Fé for Taos shortly after my arrival from El Paso, and obtained employ-

reticent on proper occasions for silence, but if he had actually wielded the surgeon's saw and razor on Broadus, he would in all probability have recorded the fact in his autobiography.

ment as a cook with Mr. Ewing Young,[5] my
board being the remuneration. In the spring
of 1828 I once more departed for the States,
met a party on the Arkansas, and again
returned to Santa Fé. I then was employed

[5] Ewing Young was a native of Knox County, Tennes-
see, where he learned the trade of cabinet maker. Sometime in the early twenties he found his way to Santa
Fé, and by 1826 was organizing parties to trap in the
Mexican Southwest. The probability that James Ohio
Pattie, whose entertaining narrative constitutes *The
Lakeside Classics* volume for 1930, was for a time a
follower of Young, and that an important portion of
his narrative in reality describes the experiences of one
of Young's parties, is suggested in the present Editor's
historical introduction to that volume, pp. xxi–xxii.
In the latter half of 1829, Young led an expedition (of
which Carson was a member) from Taos to California.
Its experiences, until the return to Taos in the spring
of 1831, are recited by Carson in the succeeding pages
of the present volume. Young soon returned to California, where in 1834 he encountered Hall J. Kelly, a
New England enthusiast who had conceived a project
for the colonization of Oregon, and the two men journeyed northward to Oregon, driving a considerable herd
of horses and mules and accompanied at least part of
the way by a band of horse thieves. The remainder of
Young's life was identified with the Willamette Valley,
where he developed a great ranch and soon became the
wealthiest and perhaps the most influential American
resident in the Oregon country. He died in 1841, apparently without family or heirs, and the situation
produced by the spectacle of his large estate in a country
without civil organization or government, was a prominent factor in inducing the settlers to take measures

Kit Carson's Autobiography

by Col. Tramell, a merchant, as interpreter. I accompanied him to Chihuahua and then hired with Robert McKnight[6] to go to the copper mines on the Rio Gila, where I remained a few months, driving a team. Not

looking to the establishment of one. Young had married a Mexican woman before leaving New Mexico, however, and a son of the marriage ultimately came to Oregon and gained recognition as his legal heir. For a sketch of Young's career, see S. A. Clarke, *Pioneer Days of Oregon* (Portland, 1905), I, Chap. 33.

[6] Robert McKnight was born in Augusta County, Va., about the year 1789. The reports made by Zebulon M. Pike (the journal of whose southwestern expedition comprises *The Lakeside Classics* volume for 1925) attracted renewed attention to the prospects for profitable trade between Missouri and Santa Fé, and in May, 1812, McKnight (who had removed to St. Louis in 1809) and nine companions set out from St. Louis for Santa Fé. On their arrival they were seized by the authorities as spies, their goods were confiscated, and the helpless captives were distributed among various Mexican prisons where they languished for nine years. Released in 1821, McKnight returned to St. Louis the following year. After vain efforts to secure redress for the wrongs he had suffered in Mexico, he returned to that country, renounced his American allegiance, married in Chihuahua, and spent the remainder of his life in Mexico. For many years he operated the Santa Rita del Cobra Copper Mine in Grant County, N. Mex., which figures prominently in James Ohio Pattie's *Narrative*, and to some extent in Carson's relation. McKnight's mining operations were at length broken up by the Apache in 1846, and he died in March of this year.

8

satisfied with this employment, I took my discharge and departed for Taos, where I arrived in August.

Some time before my arrival, Mr. Ewing Young had sent a party of trappers to the Colorado of the West. In a fight with the Indians, they were defeated; having fought all of one day, and gaining no advantage, they considered it prudent to return. Young then raised another party of forty men, consisting of Americans, Canadians, and Frenchmen, which I joined, and took command himself.

We left Taos in August, 1829. In those days licenses were not granted to citizens of the United States to trap within the limits of Mexico. To avoid all mistrust on the part of the government officers, we traveled in a northern direction for fifty miles and then changed our course to southwest. Traveling through the country occupied by the Navajo Indians, we passed the village of Zuni, and on to the head of Salt River,[7] one of the tributaries of the Rio Gila.

Here we met the same Indians that had defeated the former party. Young directed the greater part of his men to hide them-

[7] The Salido River, largest tributary of the Gila. It rises near the eastern border of Arizona, and flows westward to its junction with the Gila.

selves, which was done, the men concealing themselves under blankets, pack saddles, and as best they could. The hills were covered with Indians, and seeing so few of us they concluded to make an attack and drive us from our position. Our commander allowed them to enter the camp and then ordered us to fire on them, which was done, the Indians having fifteen or twenty warriors killed and a great number wounded. They were routed, and we continued our march, trapping down Salt River to the mouth of San Francisco River,[8] and up to the head of the latter stream. We were nightly harassed by the Indians, who would frequently crawl into our camp, steal a trap or two, kill a mule or horse, and do whatever damage they could.

On the head of San Francisco River the party was divided, one section, of which I was a member, to proceed to the valley of the Sacramento in California, and the other to return to Taos for traps to replace those which had been stolen, and to dispose of the beaver we had caught. Young took charge of the party for California, consisting of eighteen men.

We remained where we were a few days after the departure of the party for Taos, for

[8] The Verde River of central Arizona.

the purpose of procuring meat and making the necessary arrangments for a journey through a country which had never been explored.[9] Game was very scarce. After remaining three days continually on the hunt to procure the necessary supplies, we found we had killed only three deer, the skins of which we took off in such a manner as to make tanks for the purpose of carrying water. We then started on our expedition in the best of spirits, having heard from the Indians that the streams of the valley to which we were going were full of beaver, but that the country over which we were to travel was very barren, and that we would suffer very much for want of water; the truth of which we were very soon to know.

The first four days' march was over a country, sandy, burned up, and without a drop of water. Each night we received a small quantity of water from the tanks which we had been foresighted enough to provide. A guard was placed over them to prohibit anyone from making use of more than his due allowance.

[9] They were about to cross from the headwaters of the Verde to the Mohave River of California. The route taken cannot be certainly identified. For a discussion of the geographical probabilities see Charles L. Camp's "Kit Carson in California," in *Calif. Hist. Soc. Quar.*, I, 117–18.

After four days' travel we found water. Before we reached it, the pack mules were strung along the road for several miles. They smelled the water long before we had any hopes of finding any, and all made the best use of the strength left them after their severe sufferings to reach it as soon as they could. We remained here two days. It would have been impracticable to continue the march without giving the men and animals the rest which they so much required.

After remaining in camp two days we resumed our expedition and for four days traveled over a country similar to that which we had traversed before our arrival at the last water. There was no water to be found during this time, and we suffered extremely on account of it. On the fourth day we arrived on the Colorado of the West, below the great Cañon.[10]

Our joy when we discovered the stream can better be imagined than described. We had also suffered greatly for want of food. We met a party of the Mohave Indians and purchased from them a mare, heavy with foal. The mare was killed and eaten by the party with great gusto; even the foal was

[10] Apparently in the general vicinity of present-day Topock, where the Santa Fe Railroad crosses the Colorado. See Camp, *op. cit.*, 118.

devoured. We encamped on the banks of the Colorado three days, recruiting our animals and trading for provisions with the Indians, from whom we procured a few beans and some corn. Then we took a southwestern course and in three days' march struck the bed of a stream running northeast, which rises in the coast range and is lost in the sands of the Great Basin. We proceeded up this stream[11] for six days, and two days after our arrival on it we found water. We then left the stream and traveled in a westerly direction, and in four days arrived at the mission of San Gabriel.[12]

At the mission there was one priest, fifteen soldiers, and about one thousand Indians. They had about eighty thousand head of stock, fine fields and vineyards, in fact, it was a paradise on earth. We remained one day at the mission, receiving good treatment from the inhabitants, and purchasing from

[11] The Mohave River of San Bernardino County, Calif., which runs north-northeast until it vanishes in the Mohave Desert.

[12] James Ohio Pattie had visited the mission and vaccinated its inmates only a few months before the arrival of Carson's party. For Pattie's description of the mission, see his narrative, reprinted in *The Lakeside Classics* for 1930, pp. 348–49. San Gabriel mission was close to Los Angeles, which nascent metropolis the party did not trouble to visit.

them what beef we required. We had nothing but butcher knives to trade, and for four of these they would give us a beef.

In one day's travel from this mission, we reached the mission of San Fernando, having about the same number of inhabitants, but not conducted on as large a scale as the one of San Gabriel. We then took a northwest course and passed over the mountains into the valley of the Sacramento. We had plenty to eat and found grass in abundance for our animals. We found signs of trappers on the San Joaquin. We followed their trail, and in a few days overtook the party and found them to belong to the Hudson's Bay Company. They were sixty men strong, commanded by Peter Ogden.[13] We trapped down the San Joaquin and its tributaries and found but little beaver, but plenty of other

[13] Peter Skene Ogden, notable fur-trader and explorer, was born at Quebec in 1794, his father being a New Jersey Loyalist who had removed to Canada subsequent to the Revolutionary War. The elder Ogden was a judge in Canada, and Peter was given a legal education, but he turned aside from this career to enter upon the fur-trade of the Far West. About the year 1818 he was transferred to the Columbia River District. Following the union between the North West and Hudson's Bay companies in 1821, Ogden entered the employ of the latter company, continuing until his death in 1854, and rising to the headship of the company's activities in his district. For many years he was a powerful factor

game, elk, deer, and antelope in thousands. We traveled near each other until we came to the Sacramento, where we separated, Ogden going up the Sacramento bound for the Columbia River. We remained on the Sacramento during the summer,[14] and since it was not the season for trapping, we passed our time in hunting.

During our stay on the Sacramento a party of Indians from the mission of San Rafael ran away and took refuge at a village of Indians who were not friendly with those of the mission. The priest of San Rafael sent a party of fifteen Indians in pursuit. They applied to a village that was friendly for assistance and were furnished with the number of men they required. They then moved towards the village where the runaways were concealed and demanded that they be given up, which was refused. They then attacked

in the life of the region which is locally characterized as the Inland Empire. Of his present visit to California, substantially nothing is known apart from Carson's recital. For the scanty data available, see article by T. C. Elliott, "Peter Skene Ogden, Fur Trader," in *Oregon Hist. Society Quarterly*, XI, 251.

[14] The summer of 1830. Carson's memory erred at times with respect to dates, and at other times he neglected to supply them, when needed to clarify the narrative. In the present printing the Editor has supplied, or corrected, dates, on such occasions as competent editing has seemed to dictate.

the village, but after a severe struggle were compelled to retreat. They then came to us and requested our help, and Mr. Young directed me and eleven other men to join them. We returned to the village and made an attack and fought for one entire day. The Indians were routed, and lost a great number of men. We entered the village in triumph, set fire to it, and burned it to the ground. The next day we demanded the runaways and informed the Indians that if they were not immediately given up we would not leave one of them alive. They complied with our demands, and we turned our prisoners over to those from whom they had deserted, and returned to our own camp. Mr. Young and four of us proceeded with the Indians to San Rafael, taking with us the beaver we had on hand. We were well received by the missionaries.

At the mission we found a trading schooner, the captain of which was ashore. We traded our furs with him, and with the money we obtained, purchased at the mission all the horses we required, and returned to our camp. Shortly afterwards a party of Indians came to our camp during the night, frightened our animals, and ran off sixty head. Fourteen of them were recovered in the morning. Twelve of us saddled and took the trail of the lost animals, and pursued it upwards of one hundred miles into the Sierra Nevada Mountains. We surprised the Indians while they were feasting off some of our animals they had killed. We charged their camp, killed eight Indians, took three children prisoners and recovered all of our animals, with the exception of six that were eaten.

On the first of September we struck camp and returning by the same route by which we had come, passed through San Fernando, and traveled to the Pueblo of Los Angeles, where the Mexican authorities demanded our passports.[15] We had none. They wished

[15] It was the ancient policy of Spain to maintain her colonies as a closed preserve, from which foreigners were rigorously excluded. Those who persisted in coming were likely to meet with imprisonment and confiscation of property, as illustrated by the case of McKnight and his companions, noted *ante*, 8. In California, visitors by sea had begun to trickle in, and had acquired a modified measure of tolerance at the hands of the authorities two or three decades before the first overland parties from the United States appeared. Almost the earliest of these was the party to which the Patties belonged, whose tribulations are feelingly described in James Ohio Pattie's *Narrative*. The Governor whom he vilifies, José Maria de Echeandia, was still in office in 1830, and although Carson does not mention him, he was undoubtedly responsible for the attitude assumed by the officials at Los Angeles toward the Americans. For a brief note on Echeandia's career, see Pattie's

to arrest us, but fear deterred them. They then commenced selling liquor to the men, no doubt for the purpose of getting them drunk so that they would have but little difficulty in making an arrest.

Mr. Young discovered their intentions and directed me to take three men, all the loose animals, packs, etc., and go on in advance, while he would remain with the balance of the party and endeavor to get them along. If he did not arrive at my camp by the next morning I was directed to move on as best I could, and on my return to report the party as killed, for he would not leave them. They were followed by the Mexicans, who furnished them all the liquor they could pay for, and all except Young got drunk. The Mexicans would have continued with them till they arrived at the mission of San Gabriel, then, being reinforced, have arrested the party, only for a man by the name of James Higgins who dismounted from his horse and deliberately shot James Lawrence. Such conduct frightened the Mexicans, and

Narrative, 365. He is characterized by one Los Angeles historian as "a man of small ability, but apparently possessed of good intentions." In considering the conduct of the Mexican authorities on the present occasion it is proper to observe that they were seeking to uphold law and order, while the Americans were uninvited interlopers in the country.

they departed in all haste, fearing that if men without provocation would shoot one another, it would require but little to cause them to commit murder.

About dark Young and his party found me. The next day we departed and pursued nearly the same route by which we came, and in nine days we reached the Colorado. Two days after our arrival, at least five hundred Indian warriors came to our camp. They pretended friendship, but as they had come in such numbers we mistrusted them, and closely watched their maneuvers. We discovered where they had their weapons concealed, and then it became apparent to us that their design was to murder the party. There were but few of us in camp, the greater number being out visiting the traps. I considered the safest way to act was not to let the Indians know of our mistrust, and to assume a fearless manner. One of the Indians could speak Spanish. I directed him to state to them that they must leave our camp inside of ten minutes. If one should be found after the expiration of that time, he would be shot. Before the ten minutes were up, everyone had left.

We trapped down the south side of the Colorado to tidewater without any further molestation, and up the north side to the mouth of the Gila, then up the Gila to near the mouth of the San Pedro, where we saw a large herd of animals, horses, etc. We knew there were Indians near, and not having forgotten the damage these same Indians had done us, we concluded to deprive them of their stock. We charged their camp, they fled, and we took possession of the animals. The same evening we heard a noise, something like the sound of distant thunder. We sprang for our arms and sallied out to reconnoiter. We discovered a party of Indians driving a herd of two hundred horses. We charged them, firing a few shots, and they ran, leaving us in possession of the horses.

These horses had been stolen by the Indians from Mexicans in Sonora. Having now more animals then we could take care of, we concluded to dispose of them to the best advantage. We picked out as many as we required for riding and packing purposes, killed ten, dried the meat to take with us, and turned the balance loose. I presume the Indians got them.

We continued up the Gila to a point opposite the copper mines.[16] We went to the mines, where we found Robert McKnight. We could not bring our beaver in to the set-

[16] The Santa Rita del Cobra mines in northeastern Grant County, N. Mex.

tlements to dispose of, on account of not having a license to trap in Mexican territory. So we left it with McKnight, concealing it in one of the deep holes which had been dug by the miners. Young and I remained a few days at the mines, after the balance of the party had started for Taos. We then went to Santa Fé, where Young procured a license to trade with the Indians on the Gila. He sent a few men back to the mines to get the beaver he had concealed, and they returned with it to Santa Fé. Everyone considered we had made a fine trade in so short a period. They were not aware that we had been trapping for months. The beaver, some two thousand pounds in all, was disposed of to advantage at Santa Fé.

In April, 1831, we had all arrived safely at Taos. The amount due us was paid, each of us having several hundred dollars. We passed the time gloriously, spending our money freely, never thinking that our lives had been risked in gaining it. Our only idea was to get rid of the dross as soon as possible, but at the same time have as much pleasure and enjoyment as the country could afford. Trappers and sailors are similar in regard to the money that they earn so dearly, being daily in danger of losing their lives. But when the voyage has been made and they have received their pay, they think not of the hardships and dangers through which they have passed, but spend all they have and are then ready for another trip. In all probability they have to be furnished with all that is necessary for their outfit.

In the fall of 1831 I joined the party under Fitzpatrick[17] bound for the Rocky Mountains on a trapping expedition. We traveled north till we struck the Platte River and then journeyed up the Sweetwater, a branch of the Platte. We trapped to the head of the Sweetwater, then on to Green River, and then to Jackson's Hole, on a fork of the Columbia River, and from there on to the head of Salmon River. There we came upon the camp of a part of our band that we had been hunting for, and then went into winter quarters on the head of Salmon River. During the winter we lost four or five men who were out hunting for buffalo. They were killed by the Blackfoot Indians.

[17] Thomas Fitzpatrick, noted trapper, trader, and Indian agent, who has figured in preceding narratives of *The Lakeside Classics*, notably in the *Narrative of the Adventures of Zenas Leonard* (Chicago, 1934); in Charles Larpenteur's *Forty Years a Fur Trader on the Upper Missouri* (Chicago, 1933); and in John Bidwell's *Echoes of the Past about California* (Chicago, 1928). For notes upon Fitzpatrick's career see Bidwell, *Ibid.*, 24, and Larpenteur, *Ibid.*, 14.

In April, 1832, we commenced our hunt again. We trapped back on to Bear River, the principal stream that empties into Great Salt Lake, then on to the Green River, where we found a party of trappers in charge of Mr. Sinclair. They had left Taos shortly after we had, and had wintered on Little Bear River, a branch of Green. They told me that Captain Gaunt[18] was in the New Park,[19] and that he had wintered near the Laramie.[20] Four of us left our party and struck out in search of him, and in ten days found him and his party at the New Park.

We remained in the Park trapping for some time, and then moved through the plains of the Laramie and on to the south fork of the Platte, then to the Arkansas. On our arrival on the Arkansas Gaunt took the beaver we had caught to Taos. Meanwhile, the party remained on the Arkansas, trap-

[18] Gaunt was the leader of the Rocky Mountain expedition in which Zenas Leonard enlisted at St. Louis, in the spring of 1831. For Gaunt's activities in this period see Leonard's *Narrative, passim.*

[19] "New Park," sometimes called the "Bull Pen," lies in northern Colorado east of the Continental Divide, between the Park and Medicine Bow ranges of mountains. It is at the headwaters of the North Platte, and coincides approximately with present-day Jackson County, Colorado.

[20] The events of this winter camp are described by Leonard in his *Narrative*, 19–32.

ping. The beaver was disposed of, the necessaries for our camp were purchased, and in the course of two months Gaunt rejoined us. We trapped on the waters of the Arkansas until the rivers began to freeze, and then went into winter quarters on the main stream.[21] During the winter we passed a pleasant time. The snow was very deep, and we had no difficulty in procuring as much buffalo meat as we required.

In January, 1833, a party of men who had been out hunting returned about dark. Their horses were very poor, having been fed during the winter on cottonwood bark, and they turned them out to gather such nourishment as they could find. That night a party of about fifty Crow Indians came to our camp and stole nine of the horses that were loose. In the morning we discovered sign of the Indians and twelve of us took the trail and traveled about forty miles. It was getting late. Our animals were fatigued for the snow was deep, and the passing of many herds of

[21] Leonard relates (*Narrative*, 85–86) that about the end of February, 1833, his party (which had separated from Captain Gaunt the year before) found at the junction of the Laramie with the Platte a letter which had been posted there by Gaunt, stating that he had left there in September, 1832, to establish a trading post on the Arkansas. Carson's statement shows that this intention was carried out.

buffaloes during the day caused us a great deal of difficulty in keeping the trail. At length we saw a grove of timber at a distance of two or three miles. Taking into consideration the condition of our animals, we concluded to make for it and camp for the night. On our arrival, however, we saw fires about four miles ahead of us. We tied our animals to trees, and as soon as it became dark, took a circuitous route for the Indian camp.

We planned to come upon the Indians from the direction in which they were traveling. It took us some time to get close enough to the camp to discover their strength, as we had to crawl, and use all the means that we were aware of to elude detection. After maneuvering in this direction for some time, we came within about one hundred yards of their camp. The Indians were in two forts of about equal strength. They were dancing and singing, and passing the night jovially in honor of their robbery of the whites. We spied our horses, which were tied near the entrance of one of the forts. Let come what would, we were bound to get them. We remained concealed in the brush, suffering severely from the cold, until the Indians laid down to sleep.

When we thought they were all asleep, six of us crawled towards our animals, the rest remaining where they were as a reserve for us to fall back on in case we did not meet with success. We hid behind logs and crawled silently towards the fort, the snow being of great service to us for when crawling we were not liable to make any noise. We finally reached the horses, cut the ropes, and by throwing snow balls at them drove them to where our reserve was stationed. We then held a council, taking the views of each in regard to what had best be done. Some were in favor of retiring; having recovered their property and received no damage, they were willing to return to camp. Not so with those that had lost no animals. They wanted satisfaction for the trouble and hardships they had gone through while in pursuit of the thieves. Myself and two others were the only ones that had not lost horses and we were determined to have satisfaction, let the consequences be ever so fatal. The peace party could not get a convert to their side. Seeing us so determined to fight (there is always a brotherly affection existing among trappers and the side of danger is always their choice), it was not long before all agreed to join us in our perilous enterprise.

We started the horses that had been re-taken to the place where we had tied our other animals, with three of our men acting

as an escort. We then marched directly for
the fort from which we had taken our horses.
When we were within a few paces of it, a dog
discovered us and began to bark. The Indians were alarmed and commenced to get
up, when we opened a deadly fire, each ball
taking its victim. We killed nearly every
Indian in the fort. The few that remained
were wounded and made their escape to the
other fort, whose inmates commenced firing
on us, but without any effect, since we kept
concealed behind trees, firing only when we
were sure of our object. It was now near
day, and the Indians could see our force,
which was so weak they concluded to charge
on us. We received them calmly, and when
they got very close fired on them, killing five,
and the balance returned to their fort. After
some deliberation among themselves, they
finally made another attempt, which met
with greater success. We had to retreat, but
there was much timber in the vicinity, and
we had but little difficulty in making our
camp, where, being reinforced by the three
men with the horses, we awaited the approach
of the enemy. Since they did not attack us,
we started for our main camp and arrived
there in the evening. During our pursuit of
the lost animals we suffered considerably,
but in the success of recovering our horses

and sending many a redskin to his long home, our sufferings were soon forgotten.[22] We remained in our camp without any further molestation until spring,[23] when we started for Laramie River on another trapping expedition.

Before our departure we cached what beaver we had on hand, some four hundred pounds. When we arrived on the south fork of the Platte, two of our men deserted, taking with them three of our best animals. We suspected their design, and Gaunt sent myself and another man in pursuit. They had a day the start and we could not overtake them. When we arrived at our old camp, we discovered that they had raised the beaver and taken it down the Arkansas in a canoe which we had made during the winter for the purpose of crossing the river. The men and the beaver we never heard of again. I pre-

[22] George B. Grinnell, "Bent's Old Fort and Its Builders," in *Kansas Hist. Colls.*, Vol. XV, records the story of the fight as related by Black Whiteman. Whiteman was one of two Cheyenne Indians who accompanied Carson's party, and the Cheyenne tradition of the fight, as reported by them, states that only two Crows were slain by the trappers. Although the Cheyenne twitted Carson about his failure to kill more, they bestowed upon him the title "Little Chief." See Stanley Vestal, *Kit Carson, the Happy Warrior of the Old West* (Boston and N. Y., 1928), 67-71.

[23] The spring of 1833.

sume they were killed by Indians. They deserved such a fate for their dishonesty. We recovered the stolen animals and considered ourselves fortunate, as they were of much more service to us than men that we could never trust again.

We took possession of one of the buildings that had been built during the winter and made the necessary preparations for our defense, not having the remotest idea how long we should have to remain. Being by ourselves we never ventured very far from our fort, unless for the purpose of procuring meat. We kept our horses picketed near, and at night slept in the house, always keeping a good lookout so that we might not be surprised when unprepared. We were here about a month when Mr. Blackwell, Gaunt's partner, arrived from the States, accompanied by ten or fifteen men. Shortly after their arrival four trappers of Gaunt's party arrived. They had been sent to find us and learn whether we were dead or alive, the former being the general belief.

We remained only a few days after the arrival of the trappers. They stated that Gaunt's camp was in the Balla Salado,[24] the headwaters of the South Fork of the Platte.

[24] The Bayou Salade, now known as South Park, is a high valley about thirty by forty miles in area and

While we were eating breakfast on the fourth day of our march, we discovered a party of Indians trying to steal our horses. Suspecting no danger, we had turned them out to graze, some hobbled and some loose. As soon as we perceived the Indians we made for them. One Indian was killed, and the rest ran away. They stole only one horse from us, one of the Indians having been lucky enough to mount one of the loose horses and make his escape.

We traveled about fifty miles that day and thought that we had got clear of the Indians. We camped on a beautiful stream, one of the tributaries of the Arkansas. During the night we staked our best animals. We had a very watchful dog with us and during the night he kept barking continually. We were aware of the Indians being close

having an elevation of 8,000 to 10,000 feet, lying east of the Continental Divide, between the South Platte and the North Fork of the South Platte, largely in Park County, Colorado. Its early name was derived from the presence of salt springs which made the park a favorite resort for buffalo and other animals. Major Pike entered the southern portion of the park in 1806–7. Thereafter it was visited by trappers more or less frequently, but was not known to the outside world until advertised by Frémont, who crossed it in 1844. See Reuben G. Thwaites (ed.), *Early Western Travels*, 1748–1846, Vol. XV, 292, and Vol. XXVIII, 199; George F. Ruxton, *Life in the Far West* (N. Y., 1849), 41.

and kept good watch. In the morning myself and three others proposed to go to a fork of the river that we knew of. It was not far, and we wished to visit it to look for beaver sign. If they were good we intended to trap the stream; if not, to proceed on our journey.

About an hour after we left, a large party of Indians charged the camp, running off all the loose animals. Four of our men immediately mounted four of the best animals and followed them. In a short time they overtook the Indians and recaptured all of the animals. One of the men was severely wounded in the affray, and one Indian was killed.

The route which we had to follow to reach the fork led over a mountain that was difficult to pass. After some trouble, we crossed it and arrived at our destination, but found no beaver sign. On our return we took a different route from that by which we had come. As we got around the mountain and were near our former trail, I saw in the distance four Indians. I proposed to charge them. All were willing, and we started for them, but when we got near we found we had caught a tartar. There were upwards of sixty Indians in the band. They had surrounded us and our only chance to save our lives was by instant flight. We fled, the Indians firing on us from all directions. We ran the gauntlet for about two hundred yards, the Indians being often as close to us as twenty yards. We dared not fire, not knowing what moment our horses might be shot under us, and the idea of finding oneself left afoot with his gun unloaded, was enough to make any man retain the shot in his gun. We finally made our escape and rejoined the party at the camp. One of our men was severely wounded, this being the only damage we received.

On our arrival at camp we were informed of what had transpired during our absence. It was then easy enough to account for the Indians having followed us. They saw us leave camp and as they had had the misfortune to lose the animals they had stolen, they intended to have our scalps. They made a very good attempt, but, thank God! failed.

We built a fort and remained encamped for the night, as we could not move until the wounded men were properly cared for. In the morning we made a litter to carry one of them (the other could ride horseback) and then pursued our course and in four days' march we found Gaunt. We remained at his camp until our wounded men recovered, and then started for the Old Park. We found beaver scarce, so many trappers having been there before us.

I and two others concluded to leave the party and hunt on our own hook. We trapped nearly all the streams within the mountains, keeping away from the plains from fear of danger. We had very good luck, and having caught a great amount of beaver we started for Taos to dispose of it and have the pleasure of spending the money that had caused us so much danger and hardship to earn. We arrived at Taos in October, 1833, where we disposed of our beaver for a good sum, and everything of mountain life was forgotten for the time.

In Taos, I met Captain Lee[25] of the U.S.A., who was a partner of Bent[26] and St. Vrain

[25] Stephen Louis Lee. In 1847, while sheriff of Taos County, he was slain by a mob of Indians, seeking to release two of their number who were in confinement for stealing. After killing Lee and the Mexican prefect of Taos, the mob, now composed of both Mexicans and Indians, assaulted the home of Governor Bent and murdered him.

[26] Charles Bent, born at Charleston, W. Va., Nov. 11, 1799. He removed with his parents to St. Louis in childhood. In the early twenties, Bent entered upon the fur trade, and in 1824 Charles and his younger brother, William, accompanied Ceran St. Vrain to the Arkansas, and built a stockade on the site of Pueblo, Colo. A couple of years later St. Vrain and the Bents extended

and had purchased goods to trade with the trappers. I joined him, and in the latter part of October we started for the mountains to their activities to New Mexico, and in 1828 they organized the firm of Bent and St. Vrain and established Bent's Fort on the Arkansas, near present-day La Junta. Bent's Fort became a famous fur-trade center, intimately associated with the career of Carson. After its completion in 1832, Charles Bent and St. Vrain made their homes in New Mexico, while William Bent and two younger brothers (George and Robert) conducted the business at Bent's Fort. In 1835 Charles married Maria Ignacia Jaramillo and established his home at Taos. Carson later married Josepha, a younger sister of Mrs. Bent. In September, 1846, General Kearny appointed Charles Bent civil governor of New Mexico. In January following, he visited Taos to remove his family to Santa Fé, the capital, and on January 19 was slain in his home by a faction of Mexicans and Indians who were seeking to restore Mexican rule. Mrs. Bent and Mrs. Carson were in the home, but were spared by the slayers.

Bent's Fort (named Fort William at first) became the most important fur-trade center of the Rocky Mountains area. It was a massive enclosure of adobe construction with walls seventeen feet high and six feet through at the base. During the years of its glory it was a rendezvous of both red and white men from over a wide area. In the late forties William Bent proposed to sell the fort to the Government, but his price was not met and in the summer of 1849 he destroyed the fort by fire and explosion combined. He died at Las Animas, Colo., May 19, 1869. He outlived two Cheyenne wives, and in old age married the half-breed daughter of Alexander Harvey, who figures prominently in Charles Larpenteur's *Forty Years a Fur Trader*.

find them. We followed the Spanish Trail[27]
that leads to California till we struck White
River, went down it till we struck Green
River, and crossed from Green to the Win-
ty,[28] one of its tributaries, where we found
Mr. Robidoux.[29] He had a party of some

[27] The Spanish Trail from Taos and Santa Fé to
southern California was developed about the year 1830,
and was in more or less constant use thereafter until
the economic and other developments accompanying
the American conquest of California and the Southwest caused its abandonment. From the Rio Grande
the Spanish Trail led northwestwardly to the Wasatch
Mountain Range in central Utah and then in a southwestern direction to the Mohave River, and across the
San Bernardino Desert to Los Angeles. A map of the
trail and a history of its rise and decline is supplied by
Eleanor Lawrence in *Calif. Hist. Soc. Quar.*, X, 27–39.
See, also, George D. Brewerton, *Overland with Kit
Carson, A Narrative of the Old Spanish Trail in 1848*
(New York, 1930), 7 ff.

[28] The Uinta River of northeastern Utah. It rises in
the Uinta Mountains and flows southeastwardly to its
junction with the Green, in present-day Uinta County.

[29] Antoine Robidoux was a brother of Joseph Robidoux, merchant and fur-trader, who is noted in John
Bidwell's *Echoes of the Past*, 13. Originally from St.
Louis, Joseph established a trading post at the site of
St. Joseph, Mo., and became the founder of that city.
Antoine was born at St. Louis, Sept. 22, 1794. He engaged in the southwest fur trade, and in 1828 married
Carmel Benevides of Santa Fé. He had a trading post
at Taos for a time, and others in Colorado and Utah in
subsequent years. He established Fort Robidoux (also
called Winty or Uinta) near present-day White-rocks,

twenty men that were trapping and trading.

The snow was now commencing to fall and we concluded to go into winter quarters. We found a place at the mouth of the Winty that answered every purpose. During the winter a California Indian of Mr. Robidoux's party ran off with six animals, some of them being worth two hundred dollars per head. Robidoux came to me and requested that I should pursue him. I spoke to Captain Lee and he informed me that I might use my pleasure. There was a Utah village close by, and I got one of the Indians to accompany me. We were furnished with two fine animals and took the trail of the runaway, who had gone down the river, his object being to reach California.

After traveling about one hundred miles the animal of the Indian gave out and he would not accompany me any farther. I was determined not to give up the chase and continued the pursuit and in thirty miles overtook the Indian with the horses. Seeing me by myself, he showed fight and I was under

Uinta County, Utah, late in 1831, and occupied it until it was destroyed by Indian attack in 1844. See Albert B. Reagan, "Forts Robidoux and Kit Carson," in *New Mexico Hist. Rev.*, X, 121–32. He served General Kearny as interpreter during the latter's occupation of New Mexico and California in 1846–47. He died at St. Joseph, Aug. 29, 1860.

the necessity of killing him. I recovered the horses, and returned to our camp, arriving in a few days without any further trouble.

Some trappers came to our camp[30] and informed us that Fitzpatrick and Bridger were encamped on the Snake River. In March, 1834, we struck out for the purpose of finding their camp, and in fifteen days succeeded. Captain Lee sold his goods to Fitzpatrick and agreed to accept his pay in beaver. Lee then started for Taos, and I joined Fitzpatrick and remained with him one month. He had a great many men in his employ, and I thought it best to take three of them and go on a hunt by ourselves. We passed the summer trapping on the head of the Laramie and its tributaries, keeping to the mountains, our party being too weak to venture on the plains.

One evening, when we were en route to rejoin Bridger's party, after I had selected

[30]The remains of this camp, occupied by Carson's party in the winter of 1833–34 can still be seen "on the east side of Green River, about a mile opposite (southeast of) the mouth of the Duchesne, the then Winty River." See Reagan's article in *New Mexico Hist. Rev.*, X, 130–31, for identification of the site and description of the remains. The author errs, however, concerning the date of Carson's occupancy of the place.

For James Bridger, famous mountain man, scout, and trader, see Larpenteur's *Forty Years a Fur Trader*, 181.

the camp for the night, I gave my horse to one of the men and started on foot to kill something for supper, not having a particle of anything eatable on hand. I had gone about a mile when I discovered some elk on the side of a ridge. I shot one and immediately after the discharge of my gun I heard a noise in my rear. I turned around and saw two very large grizzly bears making for me. My gun was unloaded and I could not possibly reload it in time to fire. There were some trees at a short distance, and I made for them, the bears after me. As I got to one of them, I had to drop my gun, and make all haste to ascend it. I got up some ten or fifteen feet, where I had to remain till the bears found it convenient to leave. One remained but a short while, the other stayed for some time and with his paws nearly uprooted the small aspen trees that grew around the tree which I had ascended. He made several attempts at the tree in which I was perched, but as he could do no damage, he finally concluded to leave. I was heartily pleased at this, never having been so badly scared in my life. I remained in the tree for some time longer, and when I considered the bears far enough off, I descended and made for my camp as rapidly as possible. It was dark when I arrived and I could not send for the elk which I had killed, so we had to pass the night without anything to eat. During the night we trapped some beaver, so we had something for breakfast.

We remained in this place some ten or fifteen days, when Bridger appeared, on his way to the summer rendezvous. We joined him and went to Green River, the place of rendezvous, where two camps were established. I think there were two hundred trappers[31] encamped, awaiting the arrival of supplies from St. Louis. We had to dispose of our beaver to procure the necessities of life. Coffee and sugar were two dollars a pint, powder the same, lead one dollar a bar, and common blankets from fifteen to twenty-five dollars apiece.

We remained in the rendezvous during the month of August, 1834. In September, camp was broken up and we divided into parties of convenient size and started on our fall hunt. The party of which I was a member consisted of fifty men. We set out for the country of the Blackfoot Indians, on the headwaters of the Missouri. We made a very poor hunt as the Indians were very troublesome. Five of our men were killed. A trapper

[31] Among them was Zenas Leonard, whose party had just returned from California. For his account of the summer rendezvous of 1834 see his *Narrative*, 217–20.

could hardly go a mile from camp without being fired upon. As we found that we could do but little in this country, we started for winter quarters.

In November we got to the Big Snake River, where we again encamped. Nothing of moment transpired till February, 1835, when the Blackfeet came and stole eighteen of our horses. Twelve of us followed them about fifty miles before we caught up with them. They had traveled as far as they could, being delayed by the snow. In endeavoring to get the horses we fired some shots at them but could not approach near enough to do any great damage. They had snow shoes, we had none; they could travel over the snow without difficulty, while we would sink in it up to our waists.

The horses were on the side of a hill where there was but little snow, and our only object now was to get them. We asked for a parley, and the Indians agreed. One man from each side was to proceed half of the distance that separated us and have a talk. This was done, and we talked for some time, the Indians saying that they had thought we were Snake Indians and that they did not want to steal from the Whites. We replied that if they were friendly they would lay down their arms and have a friendly talk and smoke with us.

They agreed to do this, and each party left one man to guard the arms. We then met at the place where the first two men were talking, and talked and smoked.

The Indians were thirty strong. They sent for our horses, but returned with only five of the worst and said they would not give up any more. We broke for our arms and they for theirs, and the fight commenced. A man named Markhead and I were in the advance, and overtook two Indians who had remained in the rear of their party, concealed behind two trees. I approached one, and Markhead the other. Markhead was not paying sufficient attention to his Indian who, I noticed, raised his gun to fire. I forgot entirely the danger in which I myself was and neglected my Indian for Markhead's opponent. As the latter was about to fire on Markhead, I raised my gun and took sight. He saw me and endeavored to conceal himself, but he was too late. I fired and he fell. The moment I fired I remembered the Indian that I was after. I looked and saw him sighting for my breast. As I could not load in time, I commenced dodging about as well as I could. He fired, and the ball grazed my neck and passed through my shoulder.

We then drew off for about a mile and encamped for the night. It was very cold and we could not make any fires for fear the Indians might approach and fire on us. We had no covering but our saddle blankets, and I passed a miserable night from the pain of the wound, it having bled freely and the blood having frozen. In the morning we found that the Indians were in the same place. We were not strong enough to attack them, so we started for camp. On our arrival Bridger took thirty men and started for the place where we had left the Indians, but when he got there they had gone to the plains. So we only recovered the five stolen animals which they had given us.

In a few days we set out on our spring hunt. We trapped the waters of the Snake and the Green rivers, made a very good hunt, and then went into summer quarters on Green River. Shortly after we reached the rendezvous our equipment arrived. We disposed of our beaver to the traders that came up with it, remaining in summer quarters till September, 1835.

There was a large Frenchman in the party of Captain Drips,[32] an overbearing kind of

[32] Andrew S. Drips, agent of the American Fur Company in the upper Missouri and mountain areas. He was born in Pennsylvania in 1789, and died at Kansas City in 1860. In 1842 he was appointed Indian agent to the tribes on the upper Missouri, with his station at Fort Pierre. Larpenteur, whose opinion of Indian agents

man, and very strong. He made a practice
of whipping every man that he was displeased with—and that was nearly all. One
day, after he had beaten two or three men,
he said he had no trouble to flog Frenchmen, and as for Americans, he would take a
switch and switch them. I did not like such
talk from any man, so I told him that I was
the worst American in camp. There were
many who could thrash him but for the fact
that they were afraid, and that if he used such
expressions any more, I would rip his guts.

He said nothing but started for his rifle,
mounted his horse, and made his appearance
in front of the camp. As soon as I saw this,
I mounted my horse also, seized the first
weapon I could get hold of, which was a
pistol, and galloped up to him and demanded
if I was the one he intended to shoot. Our
horses were touching. He said no, drawing
his gun at the same time so he could have a
fair shot at me. I was prepared and allowed
him to draw his gun. We both fired at the
same time, and all present said that but one
report was heard. I shot him through the
arm and his ball passed my head, cutting my
hair and the powder burning my eye, the

was notably poor, has supplied a mildly favorable, and
somewhat amusing characterization of him. See *Forty
Years a Fur Trader*, 345.

muzzle of his gun being near my head when he fired. During the remainder of our stay in camp we had no more bother with this French bully.[33]

[33] Peters, who first published the story of this duel, spins his narrative out to the length of four pages, and concludes with the statement that Shunar (Carson's antagonist) "was carried to his quarters and every attention shown him in the power of his companions." Stanley Vestal, who bluntly characterizes Peters as an "ass," states that Carson rushed for a second pistol, and slew his wounded opponent with it. *Kit Carson, the Happy Warrior*, 117–27. He further relates that Shunar and Carson were rivals for the favor of the Cheyenne girl whom Kit presently married, and that Carson thoroughly hated Shunar. Reverend Samuel Parker, who was at the rendezvous, but who may not have witnessed the duel, describes the affair in such a way as to imply that Carson spared Shunar's life.

In a recent letter to the Editor, discussing the point, Stanley Vestal says: "I think there can be no doubt that Kit killed Shunar. I believe Sabin got the story from Oliver Wiggins [apparently an error]. I got it from Watan, an Arapaho, now deceased. George Bent, the best informant among the Cheyennes, told me that he had always understood that Kit killed Shunar. In the face of such testimony, I think Parker was wrong. Rough men do not tell all they know to a parson."

Whatever Shunar's fate may have been, Carson long retained a feeling of lively resentment for him. When Mrs. Benton, more than a decade after the encounter, remarked that Carson must have been in many fights, he answered that he had been in but one fight of his own in his life, and pushing his shirt collar aside he quietly displayed the scar made by Shunar's bullet.

On the first of September, 1835, we departed on our fall hunt. We trapped the Yellowstone and Big Horn rivers, and then crossed over to the Three Forks of the Missouri, went up the North Fork, and wintered on Big Snake River and its tributaries. There we found Thomas McCoy,[34] one of the Hudson's Bay traders. With Antoine Godey[35] and four men I joined McCoy, having heard that beaver were abundant on Mary's River. We trapped down the river until it lost itself in the Great Basin,[36] but found few beaver. We then went back up the river some sixty miles and struck across to the waters of Big Snake River, where we separated, McCoy going to Fort Walla Walla[37] and the rest of

[34] Thomas McKay of the Hudson's Bay Company.

[35] Antoine Godey, who served Frémont on his second expedition (1843–44), was a native of St. Louis, of French blood. Frémont gives his name as Alexander Godey. Both in his knowledge of mountain lore and in courage he was a worthy rival of Carson. Their joint exploit in attacking alone an Indian camp of an unknown number of inmates is related *post*, 82–85.

[36] Zenas Leonard had descended the Mary's River with Captain Joseph Walker's party, en route for California in the summer of 1833, and had reascended it on returning therefrom in 1834. See his *Narrative*, *passim*. It would seem that McKay's party, to which Carson had attached himself, was the next to visit the Mary's River region.

[37] Fort Walla Walla, originally called Fort Nez Percé, was built in 1818 by Donald McKenzie of the Hudson's

us to Fort Hall.[38] On our march we found no game. The country was barren, and for many days we had nothing to eat but roots, and blood which we drew from our horses and cooked. On the fourth day before we got to the fort we met a party of Indians, and I traded with them for a fat horse. We killed it, feasted for a couple of days, and then concluded our journey to the fort in safety.

Bay Company at the mouth of the Walla Walla River, near present-day Wallula, Washington. Alexander Ross, whose *Fur Hunters of the Far West* was reprinted as *The Lakeside Classics* volume for 1924, was one of the builders of the fort and has left perhaps the best description of it. See his *Fur Hunters*, 204–208. A profitable trade was carried on here for many years, gardens and farms were developed in the vicinity, and by the time the settlers began coming west to Oregon the vicinity of the lower Walla Walla presented "a homelike and civilized appearance."

[38] Fort Hall was established in 1834 a few miles northwest of modern Pocatello, Idaho. In 1836, the fort was sold to the Hudson's Bay Company, which maintained it for twenty years, finally abandoning it in 1856 as a result of the Indian war of the preceding year. Owing to the fact that Fort Hall was on the Oregon Trail, it became a well-known place of resort to settlers and travelers. For a dozen years, beginning in 1842, the post was commanded by Richard Grant, a capable officer, who frequently befriended the settlers. See John Bidwell, *Echoes of the Past*, 37; Sabin, *Kit Carson Days*, 162–63; T. C. Elliott, "Richard ('Captain Johnny') Grant," in *Oregon Hist. Quar.*, XXXVI, 1–13.

We were received kindly by the inmates, who treated us well. We remained a few days with them, then started out to hunt for buffalo, having learned that they were not more than a day's travel from the fort. We killed a good many, and returned to the fort. The Blackfoot Indians must have seen us while we were hunting, for that night they came to the fort and stole every animal we had.

We were encamped outside of the fort, but our animals were in one of the corrals belonging to it. During the night the sentinel saw two men approach and let down the bars and drive out the animals, but supposing them to be our own men turning the animals out to graze, he did not raise an alarm. We were now afoot, and had to remain at the fort for about a month, when McCoy appeared and we joined him and started for the rendezvous on Green River. He had plenty of animals and we purchased such as we needed from him.

We reached the rendezvous[39] at the mouth of Horse Creek on Green River in six days. We remained here about twenty days, when McCoy went back to Fort Hall and I joined Fontenelle's party[40] bound for the Yellow-

[39] The summer of 1836.

[40] Lucien Fontenelle was "a New Orleans Frenchman of aristocratic blood, a youth born to romance, orphaned by a Louisiana hurricane," who ran away from home,

stone. The party was one hundred strong—fifty trappers and fifty camp-keepers. We had met with so much opposition from the Blackfeet that this time, as we were in force, we determined to trap wherever we pleased, even if we had to fight for the right.

We trapped the Yellowstone, Otter, and Musselshell rivers and then went up the Big Horn and on to Powder River, where we wintered. During our hunt we had no fights with the Blackfeet, and we could not surmise the reason. Near our encampment was a Crow Indian village. The inmates were friendly and remained near us throughout the winter. They told us the reason we had not been harassed by the Blackfeet during our hunt was that the smallpox had broken out among them and they had gone north of the Missouri to escape it, so that none remained on our hunting ground.[41]

and finding his way to the upper Missouri region passed his life in the fur trade, becoming an important factor in the invasion of the Rocky Mountain area by the American Fur Company. He was "a swart, foreign-appearing man, of a saturnine temperament." He committed suicide in 1837 at Fort Laramie. See Sabin, *Kit Carson Days*, 116, where the year of his death is erroneously given as 1836.

[41] Apparently this was the smallpox epidemic of 1837 which devastated the tribes of the upper Missouri area. Larpenteur's *Forty Years a Fur Trader*, 109–12, gives an account of the epidemic at Fort Union. See also the

We remained in our camp on Powder River till the first of April, 1837. The time passed pleasantly, but it was one of the coldest winters I have ever experienced. We had to keep our animals in a corral for fear of losing them. Their feed was cottonwood bark, which we would pull from the trees and thaw out by the fire.

We had to keep the buffalo from our camp by building large fires in the bottoms. They came in such large droves that our horses were in danger of being killed when we turned them out to eat the branches of the trees we had cut down. When we broke camp we sent two men to Fort Laramie,[42] where the American Fur Company had established a trading post. They never

references cited *Ibid.*, 110. If, as all reports join in indicating, the infection was brought up the Missouri River in the spring of 1837 by the American Fur Company steamer, Carson must be wrong in ascribing its ravages among the Blackfeet to the winter preceding this event.

[42] For the building of Fort Laramie, see Zenas Leonard's *Narrative*, 11–12. The note there given should be corrected by saying that Sublette and Robert Campbell were the builders of the fort, which was first named Fort William in honor of William Sublette, later Fort John, and finally Fort Laramie. It became a United States military post in 1849, instead of 1848. I am indebted for these corrections to Mr. Le Roy R. Hafen, of Denver, who is preparing a history of Fort Laramie.

arrived, and I presume they were killed by the Sioux Indians.

We now commenced our hunt, trapping the same streams we had trapped in the fall. We traveled to the Yellowstone and up Twenty-Five-Yard River to the Three Forks of the Missouri, and then up the North Fork of the Missouri. There we found that the smallpox had not killed all the Blackfeet, for there was a large village of them in advance of us. We traveled cautiously on their trail until we found they were only one day ahead of us. Six of us then left the main party to pursue the Indians and find out their strength, the balance of our men continuing their march in our rear. We came upon the Indians as they were driving in their animals and making preparations to move their camp. We then rejoined our main party and informed them of the movements of the Indians.

We had come within four miles of their village and as we were determined to try our strength to discover who had the best right to the country, I started for it with forty men, sixty being left to guard the camp. We soon reached the village, attacked it, and killed ten Indians. We continued advancing as they retreated, and the fight lasted for about three hours. Our ammunition now began to give out. The Indians soon became aware of the fact, and realizing their advantage, turned upon us. We fought them as well as we could, retreating, meanwhile, towards our camp. They charged us repeatedly, when we would turn and give fire; they would then retreat, and we would continue our course.

As we were passing a point of rocks the horse of one of our men named Cotton fell. He was held to the ground by the weight of his horse, while six Indians rushed forward to take his scalp. I dismounted, fired, and killed one of them, and the others retreated. By this time Cotton had gotten free from the pressure on him and arisen, and remounting his horse he made the camp. Meanwhile, my horse, frightened by my fire, broke away from me and joined the party in advance. Noticing a man named White at a little distance from me, I called to him and as soon as he saw my predicament he came to my rescue. I mounted behind him and we continued our retreat, and soon reached our camp.

The Indians took possession of a pile of rocks about one hundred and fifty yards distant and commenced firing on us. We returned their fire, but finding that no execution could be done, we concluded to charge them. It was the prettiest fight I ever saw. The Indians stood their ground for some time. I would often see a white man on one side of a rock and an Indian on the other side, not ten feet apart, each dodging and trying to get the first shot. We finally routed them, taking several scalps and having several of our own men slightly wounded. This affair ended our difficulties with the Blackfeet for the present hunt.

We continued up the North Fork of the Missouri to the head of Green River when an express overtook us with the news that the annual rendezvous [summer of 1837] would be held on Wind River. We set out for the place, and arrived in eight days. Our equipments had come up from St. Louis, accompanied by some missionaries who were en route for the Columbia. There was also an Englishman, Sir William Stuart,[43] who will be forever remembered for his liberality and

[43] Sir William Drummond Stuart, for whom see Larpenteur, *Forty Years a Fur Trader*, 17-18. Stuart wandered over the West for several years apparently (Larpenteur encountered him in 1833), astonishing the mountain men by his display of civilized refinements and winning their genuine esteem by his exhibitions of pluck and sportsmanship. Sabin speaks of him as bobbing up "as usual" at the Green River rendezvous of 1836; unless Carson's memory errs as to date and place, he was again on hand on Wind River in 1837.

his many good qualities, by the mountaineers who had the honor of his acquaintance.

Among the missionaries was old Father de Smitt,[44] who is now at the Catholic University of St. Louis. I can say of him that if ever there was a man who wished to do good, it was he. He never feared danger when duty required his presence among the savages, and if good works on this earth are rewarded hereafter, I am confident that his share of glory and happiness in the next world will be great.

[44] Father Pierre Jean De Smet, famous Catholic missionary to the Flatheads, for whom see Bidwell's *Echoes of the Past*, 24, and Larpenteur's *Forty Years a Fur Trader*, 147. Carson's chronology is evidently at fault, since De Smet's first journey to the mountains was made in 1840. His second, when he was accompanied by two other priests, was made in 1841. Bidwell, *op. cit.*, 25. But there was a Protestant missionary party at the summer rendezvous of 1837 in the persons of William H. Gray and two white and five red companions. Gray had first come west the year before, in company of Dr. Marcus Whitman and Henry H. Spalding and their wives (apparently the first white women to traverse the Oregon Trail), who had appeared at the rendezvous on Green River in 1836. Gray and his party were now returning eastward. Somewhere on the lower Platte they were assailed by a Sioux band; after a battle, the three white men escaped, while their red companions were slain. The Flatheads accused Gray of treachery to his red wards on this occasion, which charge the missionaries denied. See Sabin, *Kit Carson Days*, Chap. 16.

Kit Carson's Autobiography

In twenty days the rendezvous broke up, and I and seven men went to Brown's Hole,[45] a trading post, where I joined Thompson and Sinclair's [St. Clair] party on a trading expedition to the Navajo Indians. We procured thirty mules from them and returned to Brown's Hole. After our arrival Thompson took the mules to the South Fork of the Platte, where he disposed of them to Sublette[46] and Vasques[47] and returned with goods suitable for trading with the Indians. I was now employed as hunter for the fort[48] and I

[45] Described by Dr. F. A. Wislizenus, who visited the region in the summer of 1839, as "a gulch, six to eight miles long," adjoining Green River in the northwestern corner of Colorado. Near-by was Fort Crockett (or Davy Crockett), constructed by William Craig, Philip Thompson, and ___ St. Clair. The last two were Carson's present employers. See Sabin, *Kit Carson Days*, 177.

[46] Commonly supposed to be William L. Sublette, for whom see Bidwell's *Echoes of the Past*, 34. A letter brought to light by Stella M. Drumm of the Missouri Historical Society, St. Louis, however, seems to indicate that Andrew Sublette, instead of William, was the partner of Vasquez.

[47] Louis Vasquez was a Mexican and for many years a mountain man. About the year 1832, according to local tradition, he had a trading post at the mouth of Clear Creek, just north of Denver. He later had an adobe fort on the South Platte, about a mile and a half south of Platteville, Colorado, whose ruins are still locally known as Fort Vasquez. He was a partner of

continued in this service during the winter, having to keep twenty men supplied with meat.

In the spring of 1838 I joined Bridger. Besides myself, the party included Dick Owens[49] and three Canadians. We five men started for the Black Hills to hunt. After we had trapped the streams in the vicinity of the hills we separated, Owens and myself taking one course, and the Canadians another. We made a good hunt for three

Sublette (usually stated as William L., but more recently thought to be William's brother, Andrew Sublette) at this time. About the year 1840 he became a partner of James Bridger, who established Fort Bridger on the Oregon Trail in 1843. In 1859 he was part owner of a store in Denver, which was managed by his nephew, and temporarily by James Beckwourth. At this time an editorial in the *Rocky Mountain News* (Dec. 1, 1859) indicates that Vasquez was living at Westport, Mo. See L. R. Hafen, "Early Fur Trade Posts on the South Platte," in *Miss. Valley Hist. Rev.*, XII, 336–39.

[48] That is, Fort Davy Crockett. It stood on the left bank of Green River near the Colorado-Utah state line. Dr. Wislizenus, in 1839, described it as a one-story adobe building, with three wings and without a stockade. It was maintained for only a few years.

[49] Characterized by Sabin (*Kit Carson Days*, 120) as "Carson's close companion and comrade in many mountain doings; his partner in ranching it in New Mexico after trapper days; his companion upon the third Frémont expedition, and a captain in California service during the events which followed the Bear Flag. A man 'cool, brave, and of good judgment.'"

months and then started to find the main camp, which was on a tributary of Green River. We remained with the main party till July, and then went into rendezvous on the Popoaghi, a tributary of Wind River.[50] About the twentieth of August, we started for the Yellowstone, and after trapping it and all the adjoining streams, went into winter quarters.

About the first of January, 1839, a few of our men were out hunting not far from camp, and discovered a party of Blackfeet. As soon as this information was brought to us a party of forty men started out to meet them and drove them to seek cover on an island in the Yellowstone, where they strongly fortified themselves. We commenced the attack late in the day and the fight continued till sunset, when we had to retire. We lost one man

[50] In Zenas Leonard's *Narrative*, 21, our footnote indentifies the Popo Agie River as a tributary of the Big Horn. Explanation of the seeming contradiction between this statement and that of Carson is found in the peculiarities of the Big Horn and its nomenclature. It rises in western Wyoming and flows southwestward for a long distance, then turns north to its junction with the Yellowstone. Wind River is the name applied to the southward-flowing portion of the stream, and Big Horn to the northward-flowing portion. The Popo Agie enters it just at the point where it turns north, and may with equal correctness be termed a tributary of the Wind or of the Big Horn.

killed, a Delaware Indian and a brave man, and had one man wounded.

In the morning we returned to the place where the Indians had fortified themselves, but they had abandoned it. On examining the fort we discovered that they had lost several men during the attack of the previous evening. There was much blood in the fort, and a large trail, which led to a hole in the ice, revealed to us where they had disposed of their dead. We knew that the main village of the Blackfeet was not far off. Bridger, an experienced mountaineer, said: "Now, boys, the Indians are close by, and in a short time a party of five or six hundred will return to avenge the death of those we have slain, and we will have to keep a sharp lookout."

In the course of fifteen days his words were verified. A mile away from our camp there was a large butte on which we posted a sentinel, who commanded a view of the surrounding country during the day. On the fifteenth day he discovered the Blackfeet marching towards us. They encamped on a large island and immediately commenced making a fortification. They kept arriving until there were at least 1500 warriors assembled on this spot. As soon as we perceived their approach, we commenced to fortify our own position, being confident they would come in force. Our fort was strongly built and nothing but artillery could do any damage to it. The Indians had constructed one hundred and eleven forts.[51] On the evening the last of their reinforcements arrived they had a war dance. We could hear their songs, and knew that in the morning they would make the attack. They came, as we expected, at sunrise, but seeing the strength and invincibility of our position, they fired a few shots which did no execution and finding that they could not do us any damage without charging our breastworks (which they declined to do) they retired.

We were only sixty strong, the Indians fifteen hundred, but there was not one of our band but felt anxious for the fight. We dared them to make the attack, but nothing could persuade them to do so. They retired about a mile, where all sat down in council. In a short time they arose and divided into two bands, half going in the direction of the Crow country and the other half taking the course by which they had come. We remained at our fort until spring without any further molestation.

We kept our animals in the fort at night, feeding them on cottonwood, and in the day-

[51] Thus the statement appears in the manuscript; we are unable to suggest an explanation of it.

time allowed them to graze under guard. On the return of spring,[52] we commenced our hunt, trapping the tributaries of the Missouri to the head of Lewis Fork, and then started for the rendezvous on Green River, near the mouth of Horse Creek. There we remained until August, when myself and five others went to Fort Hall and joined a party attached to the Northwest Fur Company.

We trapped to the head of Salmon River, then to the Malade, and down this stream to Big Snake River and up Big Snake. We then trapped Goose Creek and Raft River, and returning to Fort Hall, disposed of the beaver we had caught. We remained here a month and then joined Bridger in the Blackfoot country. After striking the waters of the Missouri, we discovered that there were other trappers in advance of us, and fifteen of us left our party to overtake them and find out who they were. We came up with them the same day, and found they were a party in charge of Joseph Gale, engaged in trapping for Captain Wyatt.[53] Gale told us

[52] The spring of 1839.

[53] Nathaniel J. Wyeth, for whom see Larpenteur's *Forty Years a Fur Trader*, 61. He first visited the West in 1832, when he met with failure in his colonizing enterprise, but returned a second time in 1834. Gale was one of Wyeth's lieutenants. Wyeth abandoned the Oregon country in 1836 and settled down in Cambridge,

that he had lately had a fight with the Blackfeet, in which several of his men were wounded. Among the number was Richard Owens, who had nearly recovered from his wounds.

Knowing that the remainder of our party would follow our trail, we did not consider it necessary to return to them, and having accomplished our mission we concluded to await their arrival where we were. In the morning we commenced to set our traps. The men who were thus engaged had proceeded about two miles when they were fired upon by a party of Blackfeet and compelled to retreat. They reached our camp with the Indians close in their rear. We sheltered ourselves and our animals in the brush, and opened the fight. Although we were but few in number, we had the advantage of being concealed, while our enemy was exposed to view. We fought them the greater part of the day, killing a large number of them. They did everything they could to drive us from our place of concealment, finally setting fire to the brush. All the outer fringe of brush was consumed, but that under which

Mass., as an ice-merchant. It would seem that Carson's chronology is again at fault, and that the events here described belong to the period 1834–35. They are thus dated by Sabin (*Kit Carson Days*, Chap. 15).

we remained was not touched. I cannot account for our miraculous escape from the flames, unless it was the protecting hand of Providence. It could scarcely have been anything else, for the brush where we were concealed was dry and as easily burned as that which had been consumed.

Finding that they could not drive us from our concealment, and that they were losing men every moment from the unerring aim of our rifles, the Indians concluded to abandon the attack and departed. I presume they had discovered the approach of the main party, and the fear that the firing would be heard and they would be surrounded by a considerable force, with but poor prospect of any of them getting away if they remained any longer, was the main cause of their retreat. As soon as they left we started for our main camp, which was some six miles distant. Gale, seeing that on account of the weakness of his party he could not travel in safety, joined us, and we moved on together to Stinking Creek.

The day we arrived one of our men was killed by the Blackfeet. On the same day, as I was about eight miles in advance of our main party, I saw a number of ravens in the distance, hovering over a particular spot. I concluded to go and discover the cause of the gathering, and found the carcass of a bear that had been lately killed by the Indians; the trail being fresh, and taking the course I wished to pursue, induced me to return to our party. Every day, for eight or ten days, we were fired upon and forced to return to camp. We were surrounded by the Indians, and finding it impossible to hunt to any advantage, we set out for the North Fork of the Missouri. We traveled up this stream four days, when we came upon a large village of Flathead and Pondrai Indians. A chief of the Flatheads and part of his tribe joined us and we journeyed on to Big Snake River where we went into winter quarters and passed the winter without being molested by the Indians.

In the spring of 1840, Bridger and his party started for the rendezvous on Green River, while Jack Robinson and myself went to Robidoux's fort in the Utah country, and there disposed of the furs we had caught on our march.

In the fall, six of us went to Grand River and there made our hunt, passing the winter at Brown's Hole on Green River. In the following spring we went back to the Utah country and into the New Park, where we made our spring hunt. We then returned to Robidoux's fort and disposed of our beaver and remained there till September, 1841.

Beaver was getting very scarce, and finding that it was necessary to try our hand at something else, Bill Williams,[54] Bill New, Mitchell,[55] Frederick, a Frenchman, and myself concluded to start for Bent's Fort on the

[54] Concerning Bill Williams, one of the most noted mountain men, definite knowledge is disappointingly scanty. George F. Ruxton, the young English traveler, has painted perhaps the best picture of Williams in his *Life in the Far West*, 123–27. He was a veteran of forty years of mountain life when he was put to death by Ute Indians about the year 1849. A mountain, a river, and a town are named for him.

In earlier life Williams is reputed to have been a Methodist preacher in Missouri; he later related that even the chickens on his circuit would recognize him, and when he approached a farmhouse would begin to crow, "here comes Parson Williams, one of us must be ready for dinner." Williams was highly eccentric, and possibly more or less insane. He served as Frémont's guide on the latter's disastrous expedition of 1848–49, when eleven of the party perished in the mountains.

[55] Bill Mitchell, like Bill Williams, was eccentric. Dr. Peters relates that he once joined a Comanche band, became a member of the tribe, and engaged in several fights with enemies of the Comanche. His secret motive in all this was to discover the location of a gold mine reputed to exist somewhere in the mountains of northern Texas. A vast crop of such reports is still in circulation in the Southwest, but Mitchell, like most other seekers for the elusive gold, was doomed to disappointment. When he became convinced of the failure of his search, he bade his red brethren farewell and returned to his trapper companions. During the disorders of the fifties which gave "bloody Kansas" its sanguine adjective,

Arkansas. In due time we arrived on the Arkansas about one hundred miles above the fort. Mitchell and New concluded to remain here, as they apprehended no danger from the Indians. We continued our journey to the fort, which we reached in a few days. Ten days after our arrival, Mitchell and New came in, both naked. The Indians had run off all their animals, and had stolen everything they had.

I was kindly received at the fort by Messrs. Bent and St. Vrain, and was offered employment to hunt for the fort at one dollar per day. I accepted this offer and remained in their employ until 1842. I wish I were capable of doing Bent and St. Vrain justice for the kindness I received at their

Mitchell paid a visit to the States, and in his journey passed through Kansas Territory. In the heated atmosphere of the time, he was importuned by all whom he met for his opinions on the issue of the day. When he explained that he was ignorant of the current disputes and had no opinion upon them, he was treated as a secretive and suspicious individual. Having been accustomed in the mountains to treating all white men as brothers, Mitchell was so displeased by such conduct that he gave up his intended visit and returned to New Mexico. En route, he encountered a friend, who inquired where he had been. In reply, Mitchell said that after his many years in the mountains he had wanted to see the whites again, and so had started for the States; but the sample he had seen in Kansas had so disgusted him that he had returned, preferring to be in an Indian country rather than in "civilized" Kansas.

hands. I can only say that their equals were never before seen in the mountains. The former, after the conquest of New Mexico, was appointed Governor of the Territory. In the revolution of 1847 he was treacherously killed by Pueblo Indians and Mexicans. His death was regretted by all that knew him. As for the latter, I can say that all the mountaineers considered him their best friend and treated him with the greatest respect. He now lives in New Mexico and commands the respect of all, American and Mexican alike.

I had now been in the mountains sixteen years, passing the greater part of my time far from the habitations of civilized man, and with no other food than that which I could procure with my rifle. Once a year, perhaps, I would enjoy the luxury of a meal consisting of bread, meat, sugar and coffee. The last two items could be purchased at the rendezvous for two dollars per pint, and flour for one dollar. In April, 1842, the wagon-train of Bent and St. Vrain was going to the states, and I concluded to accompany it. After visiting my friends and acquaintances, I went to St. Louis, where I remained a few days. Becoming tired of the settlements, I took a steamer for the upper Missouri.

As luck would have it, Colonel Frémont, then a lieutenant, was aboard the same boat.

He had been in search of Captain Drips, an experienced mountaineer, but had failed in getting him. I told Colonel Frémont that I had been some time in the mountains and thought I could guide him to any point he would wish to go. He replied that he would make inquiry regarding my qualifications for the task.[56] I presume the reports he received were favorable, for he told me he would engage me, paying me one hundred dollars per month.

I accepted the offer and prepared to accompany him. His object was to survey the South Pass, and measure the highest peaks of the Rocky Mountains.[57]

[56] The chance which brought Carson and Frémont together proved fortunate for both men. Until now Carson was unknown to the world outside the mountains. His work with Frémont, and the publicity which attended the Pathfinder's activities, brought Carson's character and abilities to the attention of the outside world. The two men became life-long friends, and each has left glowing tributes of the other. Of their first meeting, Frémont writes: "On the boat I met Kit Carson. He was returning from putting his little daughter in a convent school at St. Louis. I was pleased with him and his manner of address at this first meeting. He was a man of medium height, broad-shouldered and deep-chested, with a clear steady blue eye and frank speech and address; quiet and unassuming." *Memoirs of My Life* (Chicago, 1887), I, 74.

[57] This was Frémont's first exploring expedition, and the first U. S. Government exploration of the western

We pursued the course to Fort Laramie that is now traveled by emigrants to California. The autumn before our arrival at the fort, a party of trappers who had joined a village of Snake Indians had been attacked by a Sioux war-party. The Sioux were beaten, with a loss of several men, whereupon they collected a large number of warriors (about 1000 lodges) to take revenge for the damage they had suffered. There were some Sioux warriors at Fort Laramie when we arrived, and they joined with the trappers and traders to persuade Frémont not to proceed, saying that in all probability he would meet the hostile Sioux and that his party would be destroyed.

Frémont replied that he had been sent by his government to perform a certain duty, that no matter what obstacles lay before him he would continue his march and accomplish his mission or die in the attempt; and if his party were slain, his government would eventually punish its destroyers. We continued our march to the South Pass, where Frémont accomplished all of his objectives, country since Major Stephen H. Long's expedition in 1820. Frémont's objectives were to explore the Rockies in the vicinity of South Pass, through which the emigrant travel to Oregon ran, and to locate sites for military posts to protect the interests of the United States in this region.

and returned to Fort Laramie sometime in September. During the expedition I had performed the duties of guide and hunter. At Laramie, I quit the employ of Frémont, who returned to the States by the same route over which he had come out.

In January, 1843, I went to Bent's Fort, and from there set out for Taos, where I married, in February, Senora Josepha Jaramillo, a daughter of Don Francisco Jaramillo.[58]

[58] Carson carefully refrains from recording anything about his two Indian wives and his half-breed children, one of whom it had been in part his mission to Missouri in 1842 (on which he encountered Frémont) to place in school. His silence is in part explained by a somewhat touching story recorded by Frémont (*Memoirs*, 74). In 1847 Carson went to Washington bearing dispatches from Frémont, and while there was received as a guest in the home of Senator Benton, Frémont's father-in-law. Senator Benton was in Missouri at the time, and the women of his family asked Midshipman Beale (who enters our narrative later on) to discover what was amiss with Carson, whose conduct indicated that something was troubling him. The explanation was that Carson was afraid it was wrong for him "to be among such ladies when they might not like to associate with him if they knew he had had an Indian wife." Although thus embarrassed, he was staunchly loyal to his dead mate, saying: "She was a good wife to me. I never came in from hunting that she did not have the warm water ready for my feet." His "straightforward nature would not let him rest," however, "while there was anything concealed which he thought ought to be known to the family who were receiving him as a friend."

Kit Carson's Autobiography

I remained in Taos till April, when I again started for the States with Bent and St. Vrain, serving as hunter for the train. At Walnut Creek we found four companies of dragoons encamped, commanded by Captain P. St. G. Cooke.[59] He informed us that

Josepha Jaramillo, barely fifteen and reputed to have been very beautiful, possessed an excellent family background, both her father's family and her mother's being prominent in New Mexico. One of her sisters was the wife of Charles Bent, the American trader. The marriage of Kit and Josepha united the best elements of Yankee and Spanish blood and influence in the Southwest.

[59] Philip St. George Cooke was a native of Virginia who graduated from West Point in 1827, and served actively in the U. S. Army until his retirement in 1873. For many years he served on the western frontier, participating in many expeditions. In the Mexican War he served under General Kearny, and from Bent's Fort to Santa Fé he preceded Kearny's army with an escort of only twelve men. Apart from his other activities, he produced two books (*Scenes and Adventures in the Army*, and *The Conquest of New Mexico and California*) narrating his army life and experiences.

In 1925 the present Editor procured a copy of the official journal of Cooke's present expedition, and induced William E. Connelley, Secretary of the Kansas Historical Society, to edit it for publication in the *Miss. Valley Hist. Rev.* (see Vol. XII, 72–98 and 227–55). The meeting of Cooke's party with Bent's wagon train at Walnut Creek, June 14, 1843, is described *Ibid.*, 84–85. The description affords an incidental check upon the accuracy of Carson's recollections, as set forth in his autobiography.

the train of Armijo[60] and several traders was a short distance in his rear. They had about one hundred men, Mexicans and Americans, in the party and a large number of wagons. Captain Cooke had received intelligence that a large party of Texans was at the crossing of the Arkansas, waiting to overpower the train and kill or capture the Mexicans, in revenge for the treatment Armijo had given the Texans when in his power.[61]

The Mexicans concluded to remain where they were and send word to General Armijo of their predicament. The dragoons were to guard them only as far as the Arkansas, and they wished Armijo to send soldiers for their

[60] Manuel Armijo, last Spanish governor of New Mexico. For an eloquent and feeling excoriation of his character and rule, see George W. Kendall's *Narrative of the Texan Santa Fe Expedition, The Lakeside Classics* volume for 1929. Despite his somewhat extensive public career, Armijo was principally a merchant rather than a politician. After the American conquest of New Mexico, he was tried at Mexico City on charges of cowardice and desertion in the face of the enemy, but was acquitted. He died at Limitar, N. Mex., Dec. 9, 1853.

[61] The allusion is to the mistreatment of the members of the Texan Sante Fé Expedition, described in Kendall's *Narrative*, already cited. The official journal of Captain Cooke's expedition, printed in *Miss. Valley Hist. Rev.*, XII, contains the contemporary record of his dealings with the Texans, whom he forcibly disarmed. See *Ibid.*, 228 ff.

protection after the departure of the American troops. They offered me $300 to carry the letter to Armijo in Santa Fé, and I accepted the offer. I set out for Taos, accompanied by Dick Owens. At Bent's Fort I was informed that the Utah Indians were on my route. Owens remained at the fort and Bent furnished me with a fine horse to lead with me, so that if I should fall in with any Indians I could mount him and make my escape. I discovered the Indian village without being seen by the inmates, passed them during the night, and arrived safely at Taos, where I gave the letter to the Alcalde to forward to Santa Fé.[62]

Sometime before my arrival, Armijo had sent one hundred Mexican soldiers towards the Arkansas to reconnoiter for his train, and he was to follow after them with six hundred men. At Cold Springs the advance party was attacked by the Texans and all but one of the men were killed or captured.[63] The man who escaped had been lucky enough to

[62] For the official report upon this mission of Carson to Sante Fé, see *Miss. Valley Hist. Rev.*, XII, 93–94.

[63] The journal of the Cooke expedition records that the Texans related to Cooke that they had killed eighteen of the Mexicans, wounded eighteen, and captured the remainder; and that they subsequently gave the captives twenty muskets and turned them loose. See *Miss. Valley Hist. Rev.*, XII, 231.

catch one of the Texan's horses, on which he rode away to report to his general. He encountered Armijo on the march with his six hundred men, but when the General learned of the defeat of his brave soldiers his heart failed him and he returned in all haste to Santa Fé.

After waiting in Taos for four days, I received the despatches from Armijo and started for the Arkansas, taking with me one Mexican. When we were two days out, we saw a large party of Utahs coming towards us. The Mexican advised me to mount my horse and make my escape, saying that the Indians had no animal that could catch him and as for himself, he thought they would not harm him, while if they should capture me, in all probability they would kill me. I considered the advice very good and was about to mount my horse, when I thought how cowardly it would be for me to desert this man who had so willingly offered to sacrifice his life to save mine. Upon this I changed my mind, and told him that I would die with him.

The Indians were rapidly approaching with one old chief some distance in advance of the rest. He came to me with a smile on his countenance and offered his hand. I offered mine in return, but instead of taking it, he caught hold of my rifle and endeavored to take it from me. We tussled for a short time and I made him let go his hold. By this time the remainder of the band had arrived. They kept up a loud talk among themselves. Some would ride about us examining their guns, opening their pans, knocking the priming of their rifles, and indulging in other maneuvers to induce us to change our positions, that they might fire and kill us before we could return the fire. We watched them closely, determined to shoot the first one that should raise his gun. They remained around us for about half an hour; then, seeing but little hope of being able to kill us without losing two of themselves, they left. I continued my journey and in a few days arrived without meeting with any further difficulty at Bent's Fort. I was informed by Mr. Bent that the dragoons had caught the Texans and disarmed them, after which the train had continued on its march without fear, not even considering it necessary to come to the fort.

I learned that Frémont had passed the fort a few days before my arrival, and had gone on about seventy-five miles. I wished to have a farewell visit with him and started for his camp. When I arrived he requested me to join him once more. I could not refuse, and again entered his employ as guide and hunter. He sent me back to the fort to purchase mules, and I bought ten head.[64] Frémont, meanwhile, continued on to the Fontaine-qui-bouille (Soda Springs) and then to Bent's Fort on the South Fork of the Platte,[65] where I rejoined him.

[64] Frémont reached Fort St. Vrain July 4, 1843, outward bound on his second exploring expedition. In his journey up the Kansas and Republican rivers his horses had suffered so much that before proceeding farther he dispatched Lucien Maxwell to Taos to purchase a dozen mules for his use. Meanwhile, Frémont continued southward to present-day Pueblo, where he was told that the Utah Indians were hostile and that Maxwell would probably fall into their hands. It was at this juncture that Carson arrived from Bent's Fort, and was sent back to secure there the mules that Frémont needed. Of the reunion with Carson, Frémont relates: "I had here [Pueblo] the satisfaction to meet our good buffalo hunter of 1842, Christopher Carson, whose services I considered myself fortunate to secure again."

[65] Bent's Fort on the South Fork of the Platte was Fort St. Vrain, at which place Frémont had arrived on July 4, and to which, after his southward detour to the Arkansas, he was now returning. Fort St. Vrain (first called Fort George) was established in 1837 or 1838. It was an adobe-walled structure on the right side of the South Platte about a mile and a half below the mouth of St. Vrain Creek, some sixteen or seventeen miles southwest of present-day Greeley. The site today is identified by a granite marker, erected in 1911. The fort was ruled for several years by Marcellus St. Vrain, an employee of the Bent and St. Vrain partnership. Francis Parkman, the historian, who visited the place in

Kit Carson's Autobiography

Major Fitzpatrick, an old mountaineer, and about forty men, were also in his employ. We separated at Bent's Fort. Fitzpatrick took charge of the main camp, carts, etc. and went to Laramie. Frémont with fifteen men, myself among the number, struck out up Thompson's Fork. From there we proceeded to Cache-la-poudre, thence through the plains of the Laramie, and crossed the North Fork of the Platte below the New Park, to the Sweetwater. We struck the latter stream about fifteen miles above the Devil's Gate, and followed the present-day emigrant route to the Soda Springs on Bear River.

From here, Frémont set out to explore Great Salt Lake, while I went on to Fort Hall for a fresh supply of provisions. I was well received at the fort and furnished with all that I required.[66] With one companion I

1846, described the fort as then "abandoned and fast falling into ruin." It was situated on the trail leading from the upper Arkansas to Fort Laramie, and was the halfway station between the latter and Bent's Fort on the Arkansas. See L. R. Hafen, "Early Fur Trade Posts on the South Platte," in *Miss. Valley Hist. Rev.*, XII, 335–41.

[66] Carson departed on this mission to Fort Hall on Aug. 19, and rejoined Frémont Sept. 4, 1843. Frémont records that provisions were scarce at Fort Hall, having been exhausted by the demands of the emigrants, passing westward over the Oregon Trail. Carson brought him flour and a few other items, sufficient for

began the return journey, and rejoined Frémont at the upper end of the Salt Lake. We traveled around the east side of the lake about twenty miles till we could get a fair view of it. In front of us was a large island, which Frémont determined to examine. We arranged the India rubber boat, and myself and four others accompanied him. We landed safely on the island, which is about fifteen miles from the mainland. We took with us fresh water for cooking, and remained part of one day and a night. We found nothing of any great importance. There were no springs and the island was perfectly barren. We ascended the mountain, and under a shelving rock cut a large cross, which is there to this day.[67]

two or three days, "a scanty but very acceptable supply." See Frémont's *Memoirs*, 201 and 226.

[67] Frémont named the island "Disappointment," having in view its barrenness of vegetation and lack of water, but he felt pleasure in recalling that he and his companions were the first to break "with the cheerful sound of human voices the long solitude of the place." *Memoirs*, 233. The expedition to it occurred Sept. 9–10, 1843. The Mormons later named the island "Castle," and the Stansbury expedition of 1849 renamed it Frémont Island. Frémont does not record the cutting of the cross, but relates that he accidentally left on the summit of the island the brass cover to the larger end of his spy-glass, which would "furnish matter of speculation to some future traveler."

In the morning we started back to the mainland. We had not gone more than a league when the clouds commenced gathering for a storm. Our boat was leaking wind, and one man was continually employed at the bellows. Frémont urged us to pull for our lives, saying that if we did not reach the shore before the storm commenced we would surely all perish. We did our best, and arrived in advance of the storm. We had scarcely landed when it commenced, and within an hour the waters had risen eight or ten feet.

We now ascended Bear River until we got above the Lake, where we crossed to the Malade. Ascending it, we went on to Fort Hall, where we met Fitzpatrick and his party. Frémont here overtook his party and proceeded in advance, Fitzpatrick keeping some eight days' march in the rear. We started for the mouth of the Columbia, and arrived in safety at the Dalles. From here Frémont, with four men, proceeded to [Fort] Vancouver to purchase provisions, while I remained in charge of the camp.[68] Upon his return, Fitzpatrick having rejoined us, we set out for Klamath Lake.[69] Aided by

[68] "With instructions to occupy the people in making pack-saddles and refitting their equipage." *Memoirs*, 275.

[69] The objectives set by Congress for Frémont's second expedition were to journey to the South Pass by a dif-

a guide, we arrived there safely and found a large village of Klamath Indians. We had a talk ·with them, and judged them to be a mean, low-lived, treacherous race. This opinion was confirmed when we were in their country in 1846.[70]

At Klamath Lake our guide left us, and we set out for California. Our course was through a barren, desolate, and unexplored country until we reached the Sierra Nevadas, which we found covered with snow from one

ferent route than the one followed in 1842, and from there proceed to the Oregon country, thereby connecting the overland exploration of the continent with the coastal explorations already made by the naval expedition of Commander Wilkes. In setting out for Klamath Lake, Frémont was now adding a post script of his own to these original objectives. His purpose now was to examine the Great Basin, and to find a river (still popularly imagined to exist) flowing from it to the Pacific. Had he taken the trouble to examine Captain Bonneville's map, published by Washington Irving in 1837, or to read Zenas Leonard's *Narrative* published two years later, he might have saved himself the painful experience of discovering anew in 1843–44 that there was no river such as the Buena Ventura, running "from the Rocky Mountains to the Pacific Ocean" (see *Memoirs*, 298). Senator Benton, father-in-law and champion of Frémont, erroneously asserted that "all" existing maps showed the Buena Ventura as running "from the base of the Rocky Mountains to the Bay of San Francisco."

[70] For the experience of Frémont on this later visit, see *post*, 95–102.

end to the other. We were nearly out of provisions but we had to cross the mountains, let the consequences be what they may. We went as far as we possibly could with our animals, when we were compelled to send them back. We then commenced making a road through the snow, beating it down with mallets. It was six feet deep on the level for a distance of three leagues. We made snowshoes and walked about over the snow to find out how far we would have to make a road. It proved to be the distance already stated.

Upon reaching the end of the snow, we could see the green valley of the Sacramento, and in the distance the Coast Range. I had been there seventeen years before, and knew the place well. Our feelings can best be imagined when we obtained a view of such a beautiful country. We returned to the place from which we had sent back our animals, and with nothing to eat but mule meat commenced the work of making the road. In fifteen days our task was accomplished, and we sent back for the animals. Driven by hunger, they had eaten one another's tails and the leather of the pack saddles, in fact everything they could lay hold of. They were in a deplorable condition and we would frequently kill one to keep it from dying, then use the meat for food.

We continued our march, and by much perseverance succeeded in making the road. This was very difficult, for the wind had drifted the snow and in many places had filled up the path which we had made. We finally got across, however, and commenced descending the mountain. Having done so, we left Fitzpatrick in charge of the main party, while Frémont, with myself and five or six men, went ahead to Sutter's Fort for provisions.[71] On the second day after we left Fitzpatrick, Mr. Preuss,[72] Frémont's assistant, became lost. We made a search for him, traveling slowly and firing guns so that he might know where we were, but we could not find him. Four days later the old man

---

[71] Carson's restraint in describing this desperate passage of the Sierras in midwinter is worthy of remark. Frémont's party left the Protestant mission at The Dalles, Nov. 25, 1843, and arrived at Sutter's Fort on March 8, 1844. The actual crossing of the mountain range was begun near present-day Virginia City on Jan. 19, until which time the party had been on the eastern or desert side of the Sierras. The howitzer Frémont had brought along was now abandoned, and half of the horses and mules perished in the crossing, from which the explorers finally emerged on the headwaters of the American Fork, "a woeful procession crawling along one by one, skeleton men leading skeleton horses." See Sabin, *op. cit.*, 228.

[72] Charles Preuss, cartographer of Frémont's first and second expeditions.

found us. His pockets were full of acorns, and he had had no other food since he left us. We were all rejoiced at his return, for he was much respected by the party.

Three days after the return of Mr. Preuss to camp, we reached Sutter's Fort,[73] nearly naked, and in as poor a condition as men possibly could be. We were well received by Mr. Sutter, who supplied us in a princely manner with everything we needed. We remained at the fort about a month, employed in making arrangements for our return to our camp.

During our stay at the fort two of our party became deranged, I presume from the effects of starvation, followed by an abundance of food. One morning one of them jumped up, perfectly wild, and inquired for his mule. Although it was tied close by him, he started to the mountains to look for it. Some time later, when his absence became known, men were sent in search of him. We looked through all the neighborhood, and made inquiries of the Indians, but could hear nothing of him. We remained a few days vainly awaiting his return, and then departed,

[73] John Bidwell came to Sutter's Fort in November, 1841. His *Echoes of the Past*, 74–82, presents an interesting picture of Sutter's establishment and of the enterprises he was engaged in prosecuting.

leaving word with Sutter to make search, and, if possible, find him. He did so, and sometime after our departure the man was found. He was kept at the fort and properly cared for until he recovered his health, and was then sent home to the States by Mr. Sutter.

About the first of April, 1844, we were ready to start for home. We went up the valley of the San Joaquin, and crossed the Sierra Nevada and Coast Range by a beautiful low pass. We continued under the Coast Range till we struck the Spanish Trail, which we followed to the Mohave River, a small stream that rises in the Coast Range and is lost in the Great Basin. We continued down the Mohave and made an early camp at the point where the trail leaves the river. In the evening a Mexican man and a boy came to our camp. They informed us that they belonged to a party of Mexicans from New Mexico. They were encamped with two other men and two women at some distance from the main party, herding horses. The man and boy were mounted, and the two men and women were in their camp, when a party of Indians charged on them for the purpose of running off their stock. They told the men and women to make their escape, and that they would

guard the horses. They ran the animals off
from the Indians and left them at a spring in
the desert, about thirty miles from camp.

We started for the place they described,
and found that the animals had been taken
away by the Indians who had followed them.
The Mexican asked Frémont to aid him to
recover his animals. Frémont told his men
that they might volunteer for this service if
they wished, and that he would furnish
horses for them to ride. Godey and myself
volunteered, supposing that some of the
other men would join us, but none did, and
Godey and I and the Mexican took the trail
of the missing animals. When we had gone
twenty miles the Mexican's horse gave out,
and we sent him back. The night was very
dark, and at times we had to dismount to feel
for the trail. We perceived by the signs that
the Indians had passed after sunset. We became much fatigued, and unsaddling our
horses, we wrapped ourselves in the wet saddle
blankets and laid down. The night was mis-
erably cold and we could not make a fire for
fear of its being seen. We arose very early
and went down into a deep ravine where
we made a small fire to warm ourselves.

As soon as it was light, we again took the
trail, and at sunrise perceived the Indians
encamped two miles ahead of us. They had

killed five of the animals and were having a feast on them. Our horses could travel no farther, and we hid them among the rocks and continued on afoot. We reached the camp unperceived, and crawled in among the horses. A young colt became frightened, and this alarmed the rest. The Indians at length noticed the commotion and sprang for their arms. Although they were about thirty in number, we decided to charge them. I fired, and shot one. Godey fired and missed, but reloaded and fired again, killing another. Only three shots had been fired and two Indians were slain. The remainder now fled, and taking the two rifles I ascended a hill to keep guard while Godey scalped the dead Indians. He scalped the one he had shot and was proceeding towards the other one, who was behind some rocks. He was not yet dead, and as Godey approached he raised up and let fly an arrow, which passed through Godey's shirt collar. He again fell back and Godey finished him.

We rounded up the animals and drove them to the place where we had concealed our own. Here we changed horses and rode back to our camp with all of the animals, save the ones the Indians had killed for their feast.[74]

[74] Frémont in his *Memoirs* thus characterizes this enterprise: "The time, place, object, and numbers con-

Kit Carson's Autobiography

We then marched on to where the Mexicans had left the two men and women. We discovered the bodies of the men, horribly mutilated. The women, we supposed, were carried into captivity. But such was not the case, for a party traveling in our rear found their bodies very much mutilated and staked to the ground.[75]

sidered, this expedition of Carson and Godey may be considered among the boldest and most disinterested which the annals of western adventure, so full of daring deeds, can present. Two men, in a savage desert, pursue day and night an unknown body of Indians into the defiles of an unknown mountain—attack them upon sight, without counting numbers, and defeat them in an instant—and for what? To punish the robbers of the desert, and to avenge the wrongs of Mexicans whom they did not know."

[75] The further story of the Mexican man and boy whom Frémont and Carson endeavored to befriend, is one of some interest. Frémont took both of them along on his return to the States, leaving the man at St. Louis, where he obtained employment for the winter, and was engaged to accompany Frémont on his third exploring expedition. The boy, Pablo Hernandez, was taken to Washington and placed in the home of Senator Benton to be reared and educated. Although he seemed a child of much promise, on approaching manhood he developed a capacity for evil which gave promise of "nothing good" in his future career. Leaving his protectors, he returned to Mexico. The last Frémont ever heard of him was a report, after some years, that a noted bandit of California known as Joaquin was none other than the boy, Pablo Hernandez. See Frémont's *Memoirs*, 409.

We continued our march without molestation till we reached the point where the trail leaves the Virgin River. There we intended to remain a day, our animals being much fatigued, but discovering a better situation, we moved our camp a mile farther on. Here one of our Canadians missed one of his mules, and knowing that it must have been left at the first camp, started back after it, without informing Frémont or any of the party of his project. A few hours later he was missed. The members of the horse-guard said he had gone to our last camp to look for his mule, and I was sent with three men to seek him. On reaching the camp, we saw a pool of blood where he had fallen from his horse, and knew that he was killed. We followed the trail of his animal to the point where it crossed the river, but we could not find his body. We then returned to camp, and informed Frémont of his death. In the morning he went with a party to seek the body, but it could not be found. He was a brave, noble-souled fellow, and I was saddened by his death. I had been in many an Indian fight with the Canadian, and I am confident that if he was not taken unawares, he killed one or two Indians before he fell.

We now left the Virgin River, keeping to the Spanish trail, till we passed the Vega of Santa Clara, when we left the trail and struck out towards Utah Lake. We crossed the lake and went to the Winty, thence to Green River and Brown's Hole; then to Little Snake River, and on to the mouth of St. Vrain's Fork. We then crossed the mountains and struck the Laramie River below the New Park. We passed this, and went on into the Old Park. From there we moved to the Balla Salado, the head-waters of the south fork of the Platte, then to the Arkansas River at the point where it leaves the mountains, and down it to Bent's Fort. We arrived on July 2, 1844, and remained until after the Fourth, when Frémont and his party started for the States,[76] and I set out for Taos. On the Fourth, Mr. Bent gave a splendid dinner to Frémont and his party. The day was celebrated as well as in many of the towns of the States.

I remained in Taos till March, 1845, when Dick Owens and I concluded that we had rambled enough, and decided to settle down on some good stream and make a farm. We went to the Little Cimarron, about fifty-five miles east of Taos, built two little huts,

[76] Here, at Bent's Fort, Frémont's second exploring expedition ended, and the members of his party went their several ways.

put in considerable grain, and commenced getting out timber to enlarge our improvements.

The year before, I had promised Frémont that I would join him in case he should return for the purpose of making any further exploration. About the first of August, 1845, he reached Bent's Fort, where he inquired for me and learned that I was on the Cimarron. He sent an express to me, and Owens and I sold our improvement for about half its worth and joined Frémont, who employed both of us.[77]

We went up the Arkansas to the point where it comes out of the mountains, thence to the Balla Salado, thence to the Arkansas above the cañon, and up to its headwaters. From here we crossed over to Piney River, and descended to within twenty-five miles of its mouth; then to Grand River, which we crossed; then to the head of White River. We went down White River almost to its junction with Green River, crossed the latter

[77] Of this act Frémont writes: "My messenger found him [Carson] busy starting the congenial work of making up a stock ranch. There was no time to be lost, and he did not hesitate. He sold everything at a sacrifice, farm and cattle; and not only came himself but brought his friend Owens to join the party. This was like Carson, prompt, self-sacrificing, and true." *Memoirs*, 427.

stream and went on to the Winty, then up the latter almost to the mountains, which we crossed to Provost Fork. This river was named for a party of trappers led by a man named Provost, who were defeated on it by a band of Indians, all of the party but four being killed.

We traveled down the Provost to Little Utah Lake and followed its outlet almost to Great Salt Lake. Here Frémont made his camp, some distance south of our former encampment. In our front was a large island, the largest in the lake. We were informed by the Indians that there was an abundance of fresh water on it and plenty of antelope. Frémont went to explore it, taking me and a few more men along. We found good grass, water, and timber, and plenty of game. We remained there two days, killing game and exploring the island, which was about fifteen miles long and five miles in breadth. In going to the island we rode on horseback over salt from the thickness of a wafer to twelve inches.

We returned to our camp and remained a day on the south side of the lake near the last fresh water. From here Frémont sent Maxwell, Archambeau, Lajenesse, and myself to cross the desert, which I have often heard had never before been crossed by white men.[78] Old trappers would speak of the impossibility of crossing it, saying that water could not be found, nor grass for the animals. But Frémont was determined to cross. Nothing his explorations required was impossible for him to perform.

Before we started it was arranged that at a certain hour of the next day he would ascend the mountain near his camp with his telescope, so that we could be seen by him, and if we found grass or water we should make a smoke as a signal to him to advance. We traveled about sixty miles, found neither water nor grass, nor a particle of vegetation, with the ground as level and bare as a barn floor, before we struck the mountains on the west side of the lake. There we found water and grass in abundance, and kindled the sig-

[78] An erroneous belief, for Jedediah S. Smith (for whom see Zenas Leonard's *Narrative*, 109) had crossed it eastward from California to Great Salt Lake, reversing the route which Frémont was about to follow. For Smith's route of 1827, see F. N. Fletcher's "Eastbound Route of Jedediah S. Smith, 1827," in *Calif. Hist. Soc. Quar.*, II, 344-49. A party led by Lansford W. Hastings crossed the desert eastward in the summer of 1846 on the approximate route followed by Frémont, which from its subsequent advocacy by Hastings at Fort Hall and elsewhere became known as the Hastings Cut-off. Both Frémont and Hastings made light of the difficulties of the desert-crossing, which were extremely severe for the ordinary emigrant party to overcome.

nal fire. Frémont saw it, and moved on with his party. Archambeau went back and met him when he was about half way across the desert. He camped one night, and the next evening at dark he completed the crossing, having lost only a few of his animals.

We now separated again. Mr. Talbot took charge of the camp, with a man named Walker[79] as his guide. He was ordered to strike for Mary's River and follow it down to where it is lost in the Basin. Meanwhile Frémont, with fifteen men, was to pass south of Mary's River, and both parties were to meet at the lake made by Carson River.

We passed over a fine country, abounding in wood, grass, and water, having only about forty miles to travel without water before reaching the Lake.[80] We at length arrived, and awaited the coming of Talbot. In two or three days his party came in. Here we again separated, Talbot and Walker to go through a pass to our south, and cross the Sierra Nevadas to the waters of San Joaquin. Meanwhile we went up the Carson River, and having crossed the Sierra Nevada, arrived safely at Sutter's Fort. Captain Sutter

[79] Captain Joseph Reddeford Walker, whom Zenas Leonard had accompanied to California in 1833–34. See Leonard's *Narrative*, 104, *et passim*.

[80] Walker Lake.

was happy to see us and furnished us everything we wanted.

We remained at the fort a few days, purchasing about forty head of cattle and a few horses, and then started to find our camp. We went up the San Joaquin Valley, crossed it where it comes out of the mountain, and then on to King's River and up it to its headwaters. During our march, our cattle had become very tender-footed from traveling over the snow and rocks. From the head of King's River we started back for the prairie but when we arrived we had no cattle left, as they had all given out and we had to leave behind all except those we killed for meat. As we were leaving the mountains, some Indians crawled into our camp during the night, and killed two of our mules.

Next morning we started back for the fort. Through some mistake we had not found our camp, and as we had lost nearly all of our animals, it became necessary to return. The same evening we came upon a party of Indians. We killed five of them, and continued on to the fort. All of us were afoot, having lived principally on the meat of wild horses that we killed on the march. We now started for San Jose, where we remained only a few days to recruit. We procured a few animals there, and crossed the Coast Range to see if we could hear anything of our party under Talbot. At San Jose we heard that they were on the San Joaquin, and Frémont sent me with two men to meet them. We found them and guided them to San Jose.

After we had all got together again we started for Monterey to procure an outfit. When we were about thirty miles from Monterey, Frémont received a very impertinent order from General Castro, commanding him to leave the country immediately, and saying that if he did not do so, he would be driven out.[81] We packed up at dark and

---

[81] Frémont had gone to Monterey the last week in January, 1846, to call upon Governor Pico. Finding him absent at Los Angeles, he called upon General Castro and other officials, and explaining that he was on a mission "in the interests of science and commerce," met with a courteous reception and received permission to refit his party in the settlements. The message of which Carson speaks, revoking this permission, was received by Frémont several weeks later, on March 3. Whether or not it was "impertinent," depends upon one's point of view. Frémont so regarded it; but he had not been quite frank in describing his mission to General Castro, and although his men may have been "citizens and not soldiers," as he affirmed, they were susceptible of being quickly transformed into soldiers, as events were soon to demonstrate. Frémont knew that war was impending, and as a responsible officer of the Mexican government, General Castro was not without excuse in ordering such a body of armed men to leave the country.

moved back about ten miles to a little mountain, where we found a good place and made camp. General Castro followed us with several hundred men and established his headquarters near us. He would fire his big guns frequently to scare us, thinking by such demonstrations he could make us leave.

We had about forty men in our party armed with rifles, while Castro had several hundred soldiers, artillery, cavalry, and infantry. Frémont had received expresses from the Americans in Monterey advising him to leave, as the Mexicans were strong and would surely attack us. He replied that he had done nothing to anger the Mexican commander, that he was performing a duty, and regardless of the consequences he would not retreat.

We remained in our position on the mountain for three days, and became tired of waiting for the attack of the valiant Mexican General. We then started for the Sacramento River, and ascended it to Peter Lawson's, where Frémont intended to obtain his outfit for the homeward trip.

We remained here ten days.[82] During our stay, some Americans who were settled

---

[82] Frémont identifies the settler as "Mr. Lassen, a native of Germany," and describes two sojourns at his ranch, one of six days (Mch. 30–Apr. 5, 1846), and a

near-by came in with the report that there were about 1000 Indians in the vicinity making preparations to attack the settlements, and requested assistance of Frémont to drive them back. He started for the Indian encampment with his party and some few Americans near-by. We found them to be in great force, as had been stated. We attacked them, and although I do not know how many we killed, it was a perfect butchery. The survivors fled in all directions and we returned to Lawson's, having accomplished our purpose and given the Indians such a chastisement that it would be long before they would again think of attacking the settlements.

We received the best of treatment at Lawson's, and finished our outfit. We then set out for the Columbia River, going up the Sacramento and passing near the Shasta Butte. We traveled on without any molestation till we reached the upper end of Klamath Lake.[83]

second of thirteen days (Apr. 11–24, 1846). *Memoirs*, 473, 477–78. He does not mention the slaughter of the Indians. The Bancroft Library contains the manuscript narrative of another member of the party, named Martin, which Charles L. Camp characterizes as "too unnecessarily revolting to prompt repetition here." See "Kit Carson in California," in *Calif. Hist. Soc. Quar.*, I, 128.

[83] Frémont's asserted intention was to connect his present survey with the prior one of 1843–44 when he

A few days after we left, information was received in California that war had been declared between the United States and Mexico, and Lieutenant Gillespie of the U. S. Marines and six men were sent after us to have us come back. After he had traveled about three hundred miles his animals began to give out, and he had but poor hopes of overtaking us. He then concluded to mount two men on his best animals and send them on in advance. These men caught up with us on the lake, and gave the communications they bore to Frémont. Having but poor faith in the good will of the Klamath Indians, and fearing for the safety of Lieutenant Gillespie's party, Frémont concluded to go and meet him. He took ten picked men, traveled about sixty miles and came upon him encamped for the night.

He sat up till twelve or one o'clock reading the letters which he had received from the States. Owens and myself were lying near the fire, rolled in our saddle blankets, the night being cold. Shortly after Frémont lay

had visited Klamath Lake from the north, and to penetrate the Cascade Mountain Range. *Memoirs*, 478, 486. Mingled with his scientific zeal was the quite different ambition to play a stellar rôle in the war which was believed to be impending. His friendly biographer characterizes him as "obviously playing for time," in this northward excursion. See sketch in *Dict. Am. Biog.*

down I heard a noise like the stroke of an axe. Jumping up, I saw that there were Indians in camp, and gave the alarm. They had already tomahawked two men, Basil Lajenesse and a Delaware, and were advancing to the fire, where four Delawares were sleeping. They heard the alarm in time, and one of them named Crane got up and seized a gun. Unfortunately it was not his own gun and was not loaded. He did not know this, and kept standing erect trying to fire. He fell with five arrows in his breast, four of the wounds proving mortal.

The evening before I had fired off my gun for the purpose of cleaning it. In doing so I had accidentally broken the tube, and now had nothing but my pistol. I rushed upon the leader, and fired, cutting the string that held his tomahawk. Having no other weapon, I was now compelled to retire. Maxwell next fired on him, hitting him in the leg. As he was turning around, Step fired; the ball struck him in the back, passing near the heart, and he fell. The balance of his party then ran. He was the bravest Indian I ever saw. If his men had been as brave as himself we surely would all have been killed. We had three men killed and one slightly wounded. If we had not gone to meet Gillespie, he and his party would have been murdered, and the Indians were evidently on his trail for that purpose. We apprehended no danger that night and as the men were much fatigued no guard was posted. It was the first and last time we neglected to post a guard. Of the three men killed, Lajenesse was particularly regretted. He had been with us on every trip that had been made. But all of them were brave, good men. The only consolation we had for their loss was the reflection that if we had not arrived, Gillespie and his four men would have been killed. We lost but three, so two lives had been saved.

After the Indians left, each of us took a tree,[84] expecting that they would return and attack us. We remained at our posts until daylight, when we packed up, and taking the bodies of the dead with us, started for the

[84] Frémont's recital of the affair states that his men sheltered themselves behind their blankets, which they spread upon the low-hanging cedar boughs and bushes. They remained thus concealed all night. The Indian attack seems to have provoked them to an unusual degree of bitterness. When morning came the dead chieftain was recognized as the one who had given Lieutenant Gillespie a salmon a short time before. On his body was an English hatchet, and in his quiver forty arrows which Carson declared the most beautiful and warlike he had ever seen. The bravery he had displayed did not deter Carson from crushing his head with the hatchet, or one of Frémont's Delaware followers from scalping him. *Memoirs*, 490–92.

camp of our main party. We had proceeded about ten miles, when we found we could not possibly carry the bodies of our comrades any farther. We went back from the trail about half a mile and interred them, covering the graves with logs and brush, so that there was but little probability of their being discovered. We would have taken the bodies to our camp, but the timber was so thick that they knocked against the trees, and becoming much bruised, we concluded to bury them. We reached our camp that same evening and found that the men had received orders to follow our trail. We camped for the night, and the next morning we moved on a few miles, leaving fifteen men concealed in our old camp for the purpose of discovering the movements of the Indians. We had not been gone more than half an hour when two Indians appeared. They were quickly killed and their scalps taken.

Frémont concluded to return to California[85] but decided to take a different route

[85] Lieutenant Gillespie had brought dispatches from the Government at Washington to its agents in California, together with verbal messages from Secretary of State Buchanan and Senator Benton, which Frémont interpreted to mean that war was at hand and that the conquest of California was "the chief object of the President." Frémont returned to further this end, and to play "a prominent if hesitating rôle" in the conquest. *Memoirs*, 487-90.

from that by which we had last entered the
country, taking a trail that led around the
opposite side of the lake. We were now lo-
cated on a tributary of the lake nearly opposite to the place where we were encamped
when we had the three men killed. In the
morning I was sent ahead with ten chosen
men, with orders to send back word, if I
discovered any large village of Indians, and
in case I should be seen by them for me to
act as I thought best.

I had not gone more than ten miles when
I discovered a large village of about fifty
lodges, and at the same time I knew by the
commotion in their camp that they had seen
us. Considering it useless to send for reinforcements, I determined to attack them. I
charged on them, and we fought for some
time; we killed a number of them and the
remainder fled.

Their houses were built of flag, beautifully
woven. They had evidently been fishing for
they had about ten wagon loads of fish in
their houses. All their fishing tackle, camp
equipage, etc. was also there. I wished to
do them as much damage as I could, and
directed their houses to be set on fire. The
flag being dry, the fire was a beautiful sight.
The Indians had commenced the war with
us without cause. I thought they should be

chastised in a summary manner, and they were severely punished.

Frémont saw the fire at a distance, and knowing that we were engaged, hurried forward to join us, but he arrived too late to share in the sport.[86] We moved on about two miles from where the Indian village had been, and camped for the night. After encamping, Owens and twenty men were sent back to watch for Indians. In an hour he sent us word that fifty Indians had returned to camp, I suppose to hunt their lost and bury their dead.

As soon as this information was received, Frémont and six men started to join him, taking a route different from that which

[86] Martin's narrative in the Bancroft Library and Frémont's recital in his *Memoirs* agree in representing that Frémont with the main party came up in time to share in the battle. It would seem that for once Carson claimed more credit than the facts justified. In front of the Indian town was a river, which must be passed before the Indians could be attacked. Martin relates that Carson's party rode along the bank seeking a place to cross, until Kit called out "Here is a good place," and the riders leaped their horses off the bank into the river. Instead of shallow water, it proved to be ten or twelve feet deep, and all went down over their heads, wetting their powder and rendering their guns useless in the face of the enemy. Frémont and the main party came up at this moment to rescue them from this predicament. See "Kit Carson in California," in *Calif. Hist. Soc. Quar.*, I, 133.

Owens had taken, so as to keep concealed. As we neared the camp we saw only one Indian, and immediately charged him. I was in advance. When I got within ten feet of him my gun snapped and he drew his bow to fire on me. I threw myself on one side of my horse to save myself. Frémont saw the danger I was in, and ran his horse over the Indian, throwing him on the ground. Before he could recover he was shot. I consider that Frémont saved my life on this occasion, for, in all probability, if he had not run over the Indian as he did, I would have been killed.[87] We could find no more Indians, and fearing that the party seen by Owens had returned to attack our camp, we returned to it, but the Indians did not again appear.

Next morning we struck out for the valley of the Sacramento, distant about four days' march. Maxwell and Archambeau were traveling parallel with the party, about three miles distant, engaged in hunting, when they

[87] In which opinion Frémont agrees. The Klamath arrows, which had excited Carson's admiration, were steel-tipped, poisoned for six inches, and capable of being driven entirely through a man, or six inches into a pine tree. In this encounter, the odds were heavily against the warrior, who had to contend with Carson, Sagundai, the Delaware, Frémont, and the latter's splendid horse, Sacramento, which was a magnificent jumper and "not afraid of anything."

saw an Indian coming towards them. As soon as he saw them he took from his quiver some young crows that were tied thereon, concealed them in the grass, and continued approaching. When he was within forty yards he commenced firing. They did not intend to hurt him, wishing to talk with him, but as he kept up a continuous fire on them and his shots were coming rather close, they were compelled to return his fire in self-defense. At the very first shot he fell, and was immediately scalped.

We continued our march until we struck the Sacramento. In passing down this river we discovered a deep and narrow cañon ahead of us. Supposing that we would go through it, the Indians had placed themselves on each side for the purpose of attacking us as we passed. But we crossed the river and continued on our way by a different route and did not go into the cañon at all. Godey, myself, and another man, whom I have forgotten, went in pursuit of the Indians, but we were mounted on mules and they could not be caught. One man, braver than the rest, hid himself behind a large rock and awaited our approach. We rode up quite close to him before he came from his hiding place and commenced firing arrows at us very rapidly. We had to retreat, and

were kept so busy dodging arrows that we
were unable to fire at him. After we had
retreated beyond the range of his arrows, I
dismounted and taking deliberate aim, fired
at him. The shot took effect, and he was
quickly scalped. He had a fine bow and a
beautiful quiver full of arrows, which I afterwards presented to Lieutenant Gillespie. He
was a brave Indian and deserved a better
fate, but unfortunately he had placed himself on the wrong path.

We continued our march and on the evening of the next day, Step and another man
went out to hunt, since we had nothing to
eat in our camp and were nearly starving.
Before they had gone far, they saw an Indian
watching our camp. I presume he was waiting for an opportunity to steal a mule. He
was unaware of their presence, and they
gradually approached him, and, when they
were near enough, they fired. He was killed
and scalped, and the hunters returned to
camp, having found no other game. We kept
on our march to Peter Lawson's,[88] meeting
no further difficulty on the route. We then
went down the Sacramento to the Buttes,

[88] Where they arrived May 24, 1846. The northern excursion to Klamath Lake, and the war with the Klamath
Indians (whom Carson adjudged far braver than even
the Blackfeet), had consumed exactly a month of time.

where we pitched our camp[89] and decided to hunt while we awaited positive orders in regard to the war.

Meanwhile, a party was sent from here to surprise Sonoma, a Mexican military post. They captured it,[90] taking one general and two captains prisoners, besides several cannon and a number of small arms. Soon after the fort was taken, Frémont had learned positively that war had been declared. He now marched to Sonoma, and found it in the possession of the men he had sent in advance.

During our stay here, General Castro ordered one of his captains and a large force of men from San Francisco to attack us and drive us from the country. While this captain was on the march toward us, he caught two of our men who were carrying news to the settlers that Sonoma was taken and war declared, whom he brutally murdered. He found that we were anxious to meet him, and commenced his retreat. We followed him for six days and nights, but could not overtake him. He made his escape by leaving his animals behind. He reached San Francisco and

[89] Near the junction of Bear and Feather rivers, below present-day Marysville.

[90] Thereby perpetrating "the first voluntary act of war by the Anglo-Saxons in California." Sabin, *Kit Carson Days*, 259.

from there went to the Pueblo of Los Angeles, where General Castro joined him, their object being to reorganize their forces.[91]

Frémont left a strong force at Sonoma, as all the American settlers had joined him by this time. He then departed for Sutter's Fort, which he placed under military command. He left as prisoners, General Vallejo, the two Captains, and an American named Leace (brother-in-law to the General),[92] in charge of the gentleman whom he made commander.[93] He then departed for Monterey, but before our arrival it had been taken by the navy, under Commodore Sloat. A few days after our arrival Sloat left, and Commodore Stockton assumed the command.

[91] Carson's statements concerning Castro's activities represent the contemporary war-time beliefs and rumors of the American element in California and are not free from inaccuracies. The murder of the two Americans which enraged their countrymen was committed by a guerilla band not under Castro's command, and not by his lieutenant. Certain of Frémont's scouts, of whom Carson was apparently the leader, retaliated the murder by slaughtering a short time later three Californians, one of whom was an old man. See Camp, "Kit Carson in California," in *Calif. Hist. Soc. Quar.*, I, 136–37; Sabin, *Kit Carson Days*, 262; *Memoirs*, 525.

[92] Jacob P. Leese, son-in-law of General Vallejo.

[93] Edward Kern, topographer and artist of the third exploring expedition, in the place of Preuss, who had served Frémont in this capacity on the first and second expeditions.

We learned here that General Castro had made his escape, and had gone to Los Angeles to reorganize his troops. We found that we could not catch the Mexicans by following them on land, so Frémont proposed that if furnished a frigate to take his men to San Diego, he would there procure animals and drive the Mexican troops from Los Angeles. The frigate *Cyane*,[94] commanded by Captain Dupont, a noble-souled fellow, was furnished him, and in four days we arrived at our destination, and our forces were landed, 150 strong. A sufficient number of horses could not be procured at San Diego and men were sent out to scour the country and to press into service any animals they could find.

Finally we were all mounted, and started for Los Angeles. The Mexicans heard of our approach, and fled, although they were 700 strong. General Castro, the Governor, and

[94] One can extract a gleam of humor from this incident of the war. Frémont's bold mountain men, many of whom were viewing the sea for the first time, were transformed under the alchemy of Commodore Stockton's fiat into a "Navy Batallion of Mounted Riflemen." It is characteristic of their ignorance of all things naval that Carson calls the *Cyane* a frigate, although it was but a sloop. The horrors of the sea voyage to San Diego so impressed Carson that never afterward could he be enticed on board a salt-water ship.

the other officers departed for Sonora, and the rest of them to any part of the country where they thought they would not meet with Americans.

We arrived within a league of the town, and awaited the coming of Commodore Stockton, as we had arranged to do before our departure from Monterey. We were finally joined by the sailors and marines, as brave a body of men as I have ever seen. As for the Commodore, it is useless for me to say anything, as he is known to be the bravest of the brave. We took possession of the town,[95] and remained there some time, until on September 5, 1846, I was ordered to Washington as a bearer of despatches, having with me an escort of fifteen men.

I was ordered to go to Washington in sixty days, which I would have done if I had not been ordered by General Kearny to join him. When I arrived within ten miles of the copper mines I discovered an Apache village. It was about ten o'clock in the morning. They were at war with us, and I knew that if we stayed where we were we would be seen, and if we endeavored to pass them, they would also see us. So I had a consultation with Maxwell and we came to the conclusion to take to the timber and approach

[95] On August 13, 1846.

them cautiously; if we were to be seen we wished to be as close to them as possible at the moment of the discovery. We kept on our way, and were about 100 yards from the village when they saw us. They were somewhat frightened at first, but when we said we were friends, en route to New Mexico, and wished to trade animals, they were reassured. We chose a good place for our camp, where they paid us a visit. We then commenced trading and each of us procured a remount which we needed badly, as nearly all of our animals had given out. We then proceeded on our way, and in four days arrived at the first of the settlements. Upon our departure from California we had only twenty-five pounds of dried meat. At the River village we got some corn, which we parched by the fire, and did not have any other food. During our trip, we suffered considerably from hunger.

On the sixth of October, 1846, I met General Kearny on his march to California, and he ordered me to join him as his guide.[96] I did so, and Fitzpatrick continued on to Washington with the despatches.

On October 18, we left the Rio Del Norte, and on the third of December we arrived at

[96] Carson had been selected by Frémont as messenger to Washington in recognition of his capable services

Warner's ranch, and marched on toward San Diego. On the sixth we heard of a party of Californians encamped on our route, probably one hundred in number.[97] When we had arrived within ten or fifteen miles of their

hitherto. The journey, with the prospect of calling upon the President and other important officials, was a coveted privilege to Carson, and his disappointment over Kearny's action in turning the despatches over to Fitzpatrick and ordering him back to California was keen. Frémont, who shared Carson's feelings in the matter, writes: "He had been so part of all my life for eighteen months that my letters were chiefly indications of points which he would tell them at home in fulness." *Memoirs*, 568. Captain A. R. Johnston of the First Dragoons, presently slain at the battle of San Pasqual, in describing Carson's interview with Kearny wrote: "It requires a brave man to give up his private feelings thus for the public good; but Carson is one such! honor to him for it!" See Sabin, *Kit Carson Days*, 273.

[97] A counter revolution had taken place in California since Carson's departure for Washington, of which Kearny's party had become apprised on Nov. 23 when they captured a Mexican mail-carrier. The Americans had been expelled from Santa Barbara, Los Angeles and other places, and according to the letters captured the "detestable Anglo-Yankee yoke" had been broken. It was these resurgent Californians whom Kearny's force of but little over 100 men must now face.

Here, as at other places, Carson's recollection of precise dates is faulty. Warner's ranch was reached on Dec. 2, 1846, and news of the near vicinity of the California army was received Dec. 5. Hammond's reconnaissance of their camp, and Kearny's attack upon it occurred in the night and ensuing morning of Dec. 5–6.

camp, General Kearny sent Lieutenant Hammond ahead with three or four dragoons to examine their position. The party was accidentally discovered, but not before they saw the encampment, which was in an Indian village. They returned to us with the information they had gained, and General Kearny determined to attack the Californians immediately.

About one o'clock in the morning we packed up and moved on. When we were within a mile of their camp we discovered some spies who had been sent out to watch the road and our movements. We were ordered to trot, and then to gallop in pursuit of them, but they retreated to their camp in safety.

I was now ordered to join Captain Johnston, who had fifteen men under his command. We were ordered to proceed in advance of our troops, our chief object being to get the animals belonging to the Californians. Captain Moore, with part of two companies of dragoons and a party of twenty-five volunteers who had come from San Diego, was ordered to attack the main body of the enemy.[98] They resisted only about ten or fifteen minutes, and then retreated.

When we were within one hundred yards of their camp, my horse fell and threw me,

[98] The Californians, perhaps 80 or 100 in number, were encamped in the Indian village of San Pasqual,

and my rifle was broken into two pieces. I barely escaped being trodden to death, since I was in advance and the whole command had to pass over me. I finally saved myself by crawling out of the way. I then ran on about one hundred yards to where the fight had commenced. I saw a dead dragoon and taking his gun and cartridge box I joined in the mêlée. Captain Johnston and two or three of the dragoons had been killed. The Californians then retreated, pursued by Captain Moore for about three-quarters of a mile. About forty of Moore's men were mounted on horses and the balance on mules.

Two or three days before this affair we had heard of a party of Californians that were en route to Sonora, and Lieutenant Davidson and I had been sent with twenty-five dragoons to surprise them. We had succeeded and had captured seventy or eighty

about thirty miles from San Diego. General Kearny with an escort of three or four men followed close upon Captain Johnston's advance guard, and when he saw the fires of the Mexican camp in the village, charged furiously in upon the heels of the fleeing pickets. It was in this charge of twenty men upon a hundred that Johnston was slain and Carson unhorsed. The arrival of Capt. Moore's supporting force and its annihilation by the Mexicans is described with sufficient clarity by Carson. The Mexicans, better mounted and armed with lances, were clearly superior to the American dragoons in this species of fighting.

horses, from which Moore selected forty that were gentle as mounts for his men. In the pursuit, the command had become very much scattered. The enemy, perceiving their opportunity, wheeled and cut off the forty that were in advance, killing or wounding thirty-six of them. Among the slain were Captain Moore and Lieutenant Hammond. General Kearny was severely wounded and nearly every other officer of his command was wounded.

Lieutenant Davidson, who was in charge of the two howitzers, now came up, but before he could do anything all of his men were killed or wounded. The enemy also captured one of his guns by lassoing the horse which drew it, fastening the lasso to the saddle and then running off with it. They hauled it about three hundred yards and then endeavored to fire it at us, but without success. Lieutenant Davidson was now helpless. All of his men, and one of his cannon were lost and he himself was lanced through the clothing several times. One lance-thrust passed through the cantle of his saddle, and if the Californian had not missed his aim he, also, would have been numbered among the slain.[99]

[99] The Californians had obtained the victory by the use of the lance alone. Only two of the Americans (Capt. Moore and the dragoon killed in the first onset, whose gun Carson retrieved) were injured by firearms.

We finally rallied at a rocky point near the place where the advance guard had been defeated, and remained there all night, not daring to move on, and having our dead to bury. We buried them about twelve or one o'clock at night, and the next day we resumed our march.

I was ordered to proceed in advance, with a detachment of fifteen men. The Californians had received reinforcements during the night. They were now about 150 strong. Throughout the day they would show themselves on every hill ahead of us. We marched in this way about seven miles. Late in the evening, when we had arrived within about four hundred yards of the water where we intended to camp, they charged us, coming on in two bodies and compelling us to retreat to a pile of rocks about two hundred yards away on our left. After we had gained this position, the Californians took their stand on another hill about one hundred yards farther to our left, and opened fire on us. Captain Emery and Captain Turner assumed command of our dragoons and charged the enemy, routing them and gaining possession of their position, which we held throughout the night.

On the day we had the first fight, General Kearny had sent three men as an express to

Commodore Stockton at San Diego. They had now returned and had arrived in plain sight, within 500 yards of our camp, when they were taken prisoners by the enemy. On the day before, we had shot the horse of a Mexican lieutenant and taken the rider captive. The parley was now sounded and we exchanged the lieutenant for one of our own men who had been captured.[100]

The place we occupied had barely enough water for the men to drink, and we had nothing to eat but mule meat. The horses were turned loose, and as fast as they got beyond the reach of our guns they were driven off by the enemy, who had command of the water, about 500 yards in front of us. General Kearny now concluded to march

[100] The leader of this express was Antoine Godey, Carson's trapper companion, who was a member of Frémont's third expedition and who had been made a lieutenant in the little army into which Commodore Stockton had transformed Frémont's band. In the exchange of prisoners, Pico, the commander of the California army, refused to surrender Godey, who alone of the captured Americans knew what measures Stockton was taking to come to the rescue of Kearny's beaten command. The inability of Burgess, the prisoner exchanged, to inform Kearny of Stockton's plans, made necessary the despatch of a second appeal for rescue; this desperate enterprise was undertaken by Lieutenant Beale, who chose his own Indian servant and Carson as companions on his mission.

on, regardless of the consequences. About twelve o'clock we were ready, having prepared litters to convey our wounded on mule back. Observing our movements, the enemy formed 500 yards in our rear, with the men stationed ten feet apart so that our artillery could do them but little damage. General Kearny now held a council with his officers. All of us knew that as soon as we should leave the hill we would have to fight again, and in our present condition this was inadvisable. The council decided to send to San Diego for reinforcements. Lieutenant Beale of the navy and I volunteered to carry the message.

As soon as it was dark we started on our mission. To avoid making a noise while crawling over the rocks and brush, we took our shoes off, and fastened them under our belts. We could see three rows of sentinels, all mounted, and we would frequently have to pass within twenty yards of one. We finally got through, but we had to crawl about two miles, and having had the misfortune to lose our shoes, we had to travel barefooted over a country covered with prickly pear and rocks. We reached San Diego the next night, and Commodore Stockton immediately ordered 160 or 170 men to march to General Kearny's relief. They were under the command of a lieutenant, and had one cannon, which the men hauled along by means of ropes. I remained behind at San Diego, and Lieutenant Beale was sent aboard the frigate *Congress*. He had become deranged from his excessive exertions and did not entirely recover his health for two years.

The relief party lay by during the day and traveled by night, and reached Kearny the next night. The enemy fled upon discovering their approach, and Kearny now moved on to San Diego without further molestation. Here he remained about a month, until the wounded recovered. A force of 600 men led by Stockton and Kearny then started for Los Angeles, which was occupied by about 700 Mexicans. We arrived within fifteen miles of the place on January 8, 1847. The Mexicans had a good position, being in command of a hill where we had to pass the river. We had two pieces of cannon, directed by Commodore Stockton. The Mexicans withstood only a few rounds of fire, when they retreated across the river, and encamped for the night on a hill.[101]

[101] This was the battle of San Gabriel, January 8, 1847, Carson's account of which is much compressed. The American combined nautical-land force (over two-thirds of the 600 men were sailors and marines) had six cannon instead of two.

On January 9 we approached within three miles of the Pueblo, after fighting during the day.[102] Only our artillery was engaged, however, since whenever the enemy came near us Commodore Stockton speedily drove them away.

On the tenth we took possession of the Pueblo, which was evacuated by the Mexicans, who now advanced upon Frémont. He was thirty miles distant from the Pueblo. He was marching to Los Angeles with a force of about 400 men that he had raised in the vicinity, and had arrived within thirty miles of the place. The Mexicans met him, but instead of fighting him they surrendered, preferring to yield to him rather than to any other American officer.

On January 12,[103] I think, Frémont joined us at Los Angeles, where we remained, unmolested, through the winter.

As soon as Frémont arrived, I left General Kearny and joined him. In March,[104] 1847,

---

[102] The battle of Los Angeles. The fight was over at three o'clock, and the town was but four miles away; but it was "known to contain great quantities of wine and aguardiente," and fearing their inability to control their men, the American commanders determined to refrain from entering the town until the next morning, when they would have "the whole day before us."

[103] January 14, 1847.

[104] February 25, 1847.

Kit Carson's Autobiography

I started for Washington as bearer of despatches to the War Department. Lieutenant Beale went with me with despatches for the Navy Department. During the first twenty days of our journey I had to lift him on and off his horse. I did not think he could live, but I took as good care of him as possible under the circumstances we were in, and before our arrival in Washington he was so far recovered as to be able to look out for himself. I was trebly repaid for my care by the kindness and attention given me by his mother while I was in Washington.

On the River Gila we were attacked in the night by Indians, who sent a good many arrows into our camp, but without effect. As soon as they commenced firing, I directed the men to hold their pack saddles in front of them and told them not to speak a word, so that the Indians could not direct their aim by hearing us, and not to return their fire, but permit them to approach, and then use our rifles as clubs. However, they did not approach, for finding they were doing no execution they departed before morning. We continued our journey, meeting with no further difficulty, and arrived in Washington in June.

At St. Louis I had the honor of an introduction to Colonel Benton, and was invited by him to remain at his home in Washington during my stay there. I accepted his invitation, and during the time I was there received the very kindest of treatment from him.

I remained in Washington some time, receiving from President Polk the appointment of Lieutenant of Rifles in the U. S. Army, and was then ordered back to California as a bearer of despatches.[105] Lieutenant Beale went with me, but on account of a recurrence of his illness, was compelled to return from St. Louis. At Fort Leavenworth I was furnished an escort of fifty volunteers, the Comanche Indians being at war. I reached Pawnee Rock without any difficulty, and encamped about 300 yards from a company of volunteers en route for New Mexico with a very large train of wagons.

[105] Carson first called on President Polk on June 7, 1847, having waited several days for an opportunity to see him. That evening the President had a "full conversation" with Carson about conditions in California and the quarrel between General Kearny and Commodore Stockton. Next day, in Cabinet meeting, it was decided to send Carson back to California bearing messages to Kearny and Stockton, the object in view being to end the "unfortunate" controversy between them. On June 14, Carson again called upon Polk, apparently his last interview with the President. See *The Diary of James K. Polk* (Chicago, 1910), edited by the present writer, III, 52, 54, 61.

Next morning when the men of this company were leading out their horses to picket them in new grass, they were attacked by a party of Comanches and twenty-six horses and all of their cattle were driven off. The cattle took a turn towards our camp, and I was able to recapture them from the Indians. I lost two horses through the fault of two of my men, who had the ropes in their hands and wishing to fire at the Indians, let them go.

The other company lost twenty-six horses and would have lost all of their cattle if my party had not been there to assist them. They also had three men wounded. They were under the command of Lieutenant Mulony.

We continued our march and arrived at Santa Fé without any difficulty. There I parted with my escort, and hiring a new one of sixteen men, continued my journey to California. At Muddy Creek, a tributary of the Virgin River, we came upon about 300 Indians, who wanted to come into my camp. I refused to admit them, telling them that they had killed seven Americans the fall before, that they were treacherous characters who could not be trusted, and that I would not allow myself to be deceived by them. I said further that their object was to come to me under the guise of friendship and then kill my party; and if they did not retire, I would fire on them. I was compelled to fire, and one Indian was killed. The others withdrew, and we had no more trouble on the road, except that we ran out of provisions and had to eat two of our mules.

We arrived at Los Angeles in October, and from there went on to Monterey and delivered the despatches to Colonel Mason, the officer in command.[106] We remained there a few days, when we were ordered back to Los Angeles. Shortly after our arrival I was assigned to duty with the Dragoons under command of Captain Smith.[107] I passed the greater part of the winter in charge of a detachment of twenty-five men guarding the Tejon Pass, to prohibit the Indians from taking stolen animals through. Since it was the main pass through the mountains, they

[106] During Carson's absence in the East, Colonel Richard B. Mason had been appointed governor of California, Commodore Stockton had departed for Washington to submit to his superiors his defense in the quarrel with General Kearny, and the latter had also departed eastward, ordering Frémont to accompany him under a state of virtual arrest.

[107] Andrew Jackson Smith, who was graduated from West Point in 1838 and immediately commissioned to the First Dragoon Regiment, to which he was still attached. He served almost continually on the western frontier until the Civil War, in which he attained the rank of Major General. He died, Jan. 30, 1897.

were compelled to go through it to commit any depredations.

In the spring I was again ordered to Washington as bearer of despatches.[108] I reached Grand River without any serious difficulty.[109] The river was high, and I had to raft my party across. In doing so, one of the rafts, on which were six rifles and a number of riding and pack saddles, was lost. It was

---

[108] Carson set out from Los Angeles on this journey, May 4, 1848, having as companion as far as Taos, youthful Lieutenant George D. Brewerton. The latter possessed creditable journalistic talents, and subsequently embodied his story of the journey in a narrative which was published in *Harpers Magazine*, and later in book form, with editing by Stallo Vinton, entitled *Overland with Kit Carson. A Narrative of the Old Spanish Trail in '48* (New York, 1930).

It seems probable that included in the mail which Carson carried eastward was the letter which first announced to the outside world the discovery of gold in California. See Brewerton, 13 ff. The public excitement which produced the famous gold rush of the following year was incited by President Polk's annual message to Congress, Dec. 5, 1848. Lieutenant Edward F. Beale, Carson's companion on the journey to carry to San Diego the news of Kearny's plight after the defeat of San Pasqual, is credited by his biographer in *Dict. Am. Biog.*, with bringing eastward the first "authentic" news of the discovery, in a trip made across Mexico, July–Sept., 1848; while Douglas S. Watson offers still another aspirant to the honor in *Calif. Hist. Soc. Quar.*, X, 298–301.

[109] Carson proceeded from Los Angeles to Taos by way of the old Spanish Trail.

near sundown, and Lieutenant Brewerton, who was with me, and some of the men were on the opposite bank. They were nearly naked, and had to remain in that state until morning, when I sent a man over to them with an axe so that they could make another raft. They made one, and crossed the river on it, when we continued our march. Some of the men were compelled to ride bareback until we reached Taos.

About fifty miles out of Taos we met several hundred Utah and Apache Indians. They made demonstrations of hostility, and we retired into the brush, where we permitted only a few of them to approach us. We told them that if they were friends, they should leave us, as we were in a naked and destitute condition and could give them nothing. When they saw we had nothing, they left us. I moved on about ten miles where I met a party of volunteers in pursuit of Apaches. I reached Taos the next day, and then went on to Santa Fé, where I found Colonel Newby of the Illinois Volunteers in command. He rendered me all the assistance I required, informing me that the Comanches were still at war and were watching the roads in parties two or three hundred strong.

I selected my ten best men, and having discharged all the rest, returned to Taos and from there departed for the States. Keeping north of the Comanche range, I reached the Bijoux River, a tributary of the Platte, and traveled down it to within twenty-five miles of the South Fork of the Platte. Here I crossed over to the Platte, and descended it to Fort Kearny. I then crossed to the Republican Fork, and from thence to Fort Leavenworth, having met with no trouble on the march. From Fort Leavenworth I went on to Washington and delivered my despatches. Returning to St. Louis, I remained there a few days and then started for New Mexico, where I arrived in the month of October, 1848.

When I was on my way to Washington, I was informed by Colonel Newby at Santa Fé that my appointment as lieutenant had not been confirmed by the Senate and many of my friends advised me to deliver the despatches to the commanding officer and not take them through. I considered the matter, reaching the conclusion that as I had been chosen as the most competent person to take the despatches through safely, I would fulfill the duty; if the service I was performing was beneficial to the public, it did not matter to me whether I was enjoying the rank of lieutenant or only the credit of being an experienced mountaineer. I had gained both honor and credit by performing every duty entrusted to my charge, and on no account did I wish to forfeit the good opinion of a majority of my countrymen merely because the Senate of the United States had not deemed it proper to confirm my appointment to an office I had never sought, and one which, if confirmed, I would have to resign at the close of the war.[110]

I was with Frémont from 1842 to 1847. I find it impossible to describe the hardships through which we passed, nor am I capable of doing justice to the credit which he deserves. But his services to his country have been left to the judgment of impartial freemen, and all agree in saying that they were great, and have redounded to his honor, and to that of his country.

I have heard that he is enormously rich.[111] I wish to God that he was worth ten times as

[110] The stupid pettiness which so often figures in practical politics seldom finds a better illustration than in this act of vindictive meanness on the part of the majority of the U. S. Senate in refusing to confirm Carson's appointment. The idea that Kit Carson was undeserving of a lieutenancy in the American army in 1848 is one to make the gods weep. The illiterate mountain man emerges from the encounter with far more dignity than does the Senate of the United States.

[111] Frémont, who became a Californian, had purchased an estate of seventy square miles, which proved to be rich in gold deposits. The income was large from the

much. All that he has, or may ever receive, he deserves. I can never forget his treatment of me while I was in his employ, and how cheerfully he suffered with his men when undergoing the severest of hardships. His perseverance and his willingness to participate in all that was undertaken, no matter whether the duty was rough or easy, are the main causes of his success; and I say, without fear of contradiction, that no one but he could have surmounted so many obstacles, and have succeeded in as many difficult services.

I remained at Taos through the winter, and during this time made two trips with Colonel Beall,[112] who was in command of the troops, in pursuit of Indians.

Previous to his departure on one of these expeditions, the Colonel had ordered a command to cross the mountains. They ad-

beginning, and half a dozen years later, when Carson was dictating his autobiography, his former chief was reputed to be worth ten million dollars. In after years he lost his vast property and was reduced once more to poverty. Whatever his faults in other respects may have been, the testimony of Carson goes far to establish the fact that he was a superb leader of mountain men.

[112] Benjamin L. Beall, at the time of Carson's service a major in the First U. S. Dragoons. Shortly before the autobiography was dictated he had been commissioned lieutenant colonel (March 3, 1855).

vanced some distance and found it impracticable to cross. The officer in charge was advised by his guides to return to Colonel Beall's camp, as it was utterly impossible to proceed farther. He returned, and gave as his reason the impracticability of the route. Colonel Beall replied that there was no such word as "impracticable" in the soldier's vocabulary, and that nothing ought to be impossible for the First Dragoons to accomplish. He immediately assumed the command in person, and I was employed as his guide. We set out once more, and after surmounting many difficulties and passing through severe hardships, we finally accomplished the object of the expedition, and then returned to Taos. On our return, after passing through the Sangre de Cristo Pass we came upon an Apache village and captured two chiefs. The Colonel held a talk with them, in which they made promises of peace and friendship, and were then set free.

We remained at Taos until February, when Colonel Beall heard that a large number of Indians were encamped on the Arkansas. The treaty made between the United States and Mexico required our government to deliver to Mexico all the Mexican captives held by the Indians of the United

States. It was the intention of the Colonel to visit these Indians and persuade them to deliver up all their Mexican captives— peaceably if he could, forcibly if he must. His command consisted of two companies of dragoons, and I was chosen as his guide. We found four nations of Indians, some two thousand souls, encamped on the Arkansas. Colonel Beall told the Indian agent the object of his visit and was informed that it would be useless to demand the captives at present, as the Indians would surely refuse to surrender them voluntarily, and their numbers were so superior to Colonel Beall's force that he would fail in his object if he undertook to compel them.

A great deal of persuasion was required to induce the Colonel to desist from making the attempt, but as the Agent, the traders, and the officers of his command were opposed to it, he finally concluded to postpone his demand for the prisoners to some later day; especially since, in all probability, the object in view could be attained by entering into a treaty with them and making the delivery of the captives one of the articles of the treaty.

On leaving the Indians, we marched up the Arkansas to the mouth of the Huerfano, then through the Sangre de Cristo Pass, and thence back to Taos.

In April, 1849, Mr. Maxwell and I concluded to make a settlement at the Rayado.[113] We felt that we had been leading a roving life long enough and that now, if ever, was the time to make a home for ourselves and children. We were getting old and could not expect much longer to continue able to gain a livelihood as we had been doing for many years. So we went to Rayado, where we commenced building and making other

[113] The Rayado was a beautiful mountain valley, drained by Rayado River, about fifty miles east of Taos. The definite article was soon dropped from the name. Lucien Maxwell was the son of Hugh H. Maxwell, a merchant of Kaskaskia, Ill., and Odile Menard, daughter of Pierre Menard, a leading citizen of Illinois in the first half of the nineteenth century. Lucien married a daughter of Judge Charles Beaubien, and through this connection became the manager and eventually the inheritor of an immense land grant of over 1,700,000 acres, comprising the western half of Colfax County, which had been made by Governor Manuel Armijo in 1841 to Carlos Beaubien and Guadalupe Miranda. The Maxwell grant, as it came to be known, has been said to have been the greatest private estate in the United States. Maxwell resided on it in baronial style, and through his friendship for Carson induced the latter to establish his home in proximity to Maxwell's residence. Dr. Peters supplies an interesting picture of the settlement at the time his life of Carson was written in the later fifties. See pp. 331–32. Maxwell eventually sold his grant to an English syndicate in 1867 for $1,250,000. For the history of the grant, see Charles F. Coan, *Hist. of New Mexico* (Chicago and New York, 1825), I, 481–82.

improvements, and were soon started on the way to prosperity.

In October, the train of a Mr. White was attacked by the Jicarilla Apache. White was killed, and his wife and child were taken prisoners.[114] A party was organized in Taos,

[114] Probably because of the fact that the American nation had not as yet had much experience with the Apache Indians, the destruction of the White family became a somewhat celebrated tragedy, although un-counted others no less sad have marked the relations of the white men and the Apache in the Southwest. James M. White was a merchant of Independence and Santa Fé, who had been for some years engaged in the Santa Fé and Southwest trade. In October, 1849, he was traveling to Santa Fé with his wife and small daughter. White had traveled in company with the caravan of Francis Xavier Aubrey, a well-known Santa Fé trader of the period (a year earlier, Aubrey had performed the remarkable feat of riding from Santa Fé to Inde-pendence, 780 miles, in eight days, thereby winning much fame and many bets), until reaching a point where the danger of Indian attacks was thought to be past, when White hurried on in advance of the caravan, escorted by only a few men. All of the men of the party were slain, while Mrs. White and her child were re-served for the sad fate which Carson feelingly describes. Although Congress appropriated $1,500 to be used in ransoming the little girl, and the War Department pro-vided an armed escort for Isaac Dunn, Mrs. White's brother, who went in search of her, she was never found. Dr. Peters supplies a precise account of her death at the hands of the Apache and in the presence of the cap-tive mother, but his relation seems to rest on no valid authority. See *Life and Adventures of Kit Carson*, 333.

with Leroux[115] and Fisher as guides, to rescue them. When they reached Rayado, I was also employed as a guide. We marched to the place where the depredation had been committed, and then followed the trail of the Indians. I was the first man to discover the camp where the murder had been perpetrated. The trunks of the unfortunate family had been broken open, the harnesses cut to pieces, and everything else that the Indians could not carry away with them had been destroyed. We tracked them for ten or twelve days over the most difficult trail that I have ever followed. Upon leaving their camps they would separate in small groups of two or three persons and travel in different directions, to meet again at some appointed place. In nearly every camp we found some of Mrs. White's clothing, and these discoveries spurred us to continue the pursuit with renewed energy.

We finally came in view of the Indian camp. I was in the advance, and at once

[115] Antoine Leroux, a veteran mountain man, whose reputation and skill as a guide, according to Dr. Peters, was second only to that of Carson. Peters accords Leroux high praise, and states that although partisans of Leroux and Carson disputed over their respective merits, the two men were themselves loyal friends.

started for it, calling to our men to come on. The commanding officer[116] ordered a halt, however, and no one followed me. I was afterwards informed that Leroux, the principal guide, had advised the officer to halt us, as the Indians wished to have a parley. The latter, seeing that the troops did not intend to charge, commenced packing up in all haste. Just as the halt was ordered, the commanding officer was shot; the ball passed through his coat, his gauntlets that were in his pocket, and his shirt, stopping at the skin, and doing no other damage than making him a little sick at the stomach. The gauntlets had saved his life, sparing a gallant officer to the service of his country. As soon as he had recovered from the shock given him by the ball, he ordered the men to charge, but it was too late to save the captives. There was only one Indian left in the camp, who was promptly shot while he was running into the river in a vain effort to escape. At a distance of about 200 yards, the body of Mrs. White was found, still perfectly warm. She had been shot through the heart

[116] Major William N. Grier of the First U. S. Dragoons then in command of the post at Taos. He was graduated from West Point in 1835, and was retired in 1870 with the rank of colonel. In March, 1865, he was brevetted brigadier general for faithful and meritorious service throughout the Civil War.

with an arrow not more than five minutes before. She evidently knew that some one was coming to her rescue. Although she did not see us, it was apparent that she was endeavoring to make her escape when she received the fatal shot.

I am certain that if the Indians had been charged immediately on our arrival, she would have been saved. They did not know of our approach, and as they were not paying any particular attention to her, perhaps she could have managed to run towards us, and if she had, the Indians would have been afraid to follow her. However, the treatment she had received from them was so brutal and horrible that she could not possibly have lived very long. Her death, I think, should never be regretted by her friends. She is surely far more happy in heaven, with her God, than among her friends on this earth.

I do not wish to be understood as attaching any blame to the officer in command of the expedition or to the principal guide. They acted as they thought best for the purpose of saving Mrs. White. We merely differed in opinion at the time, but I have no doubt that they now see that if my advice had been taken, her life might have been saved, for at least a short period.

Kit Carson's Autobiography

We pursued the Indians for about six miles on a level prairie. We captured all their baggage and camp equipage, many of them running off without any of their clothing. We also took some of their animals. One warrior was killed, and two or three children were captured. We found a book in the camp, the first of the kind I had ever seen, in which I was represented as a great hero, slaying Indians by the hundred.[117] I have often thought that Mrs. White must have read it, and knowing that I lived nearby, must have prayed for my appearance in order that she might be saved. I did come, but I lacked the power to persuade those that were in command over me to follow my plan for her rescue. They would not listen to me and they failed. I will say no more regarding this matter, nor attach any blame to any particular person, for I presume the consciences of those who were the cause of the tragedy have severely punished them ere this.

[117] Here, apparently for the first time, the real Carson came face to face with the popular hero of the paperback novels. It must have been an interesting spectacle to observe his reactions as he listened to the reading of the book. Stanley Vestal speaks of his "naïve delight" in listening to the reading (*Kit Carson, the Happy Warrior*, 254). To the present Editor his words seem to indicate a soberer and sadder reaction to the immediate situation in which he found himself.

On the return we encountered the severest snow storm I have ever experienced. We were trying to make Barclay's fort on the Mora River, but the wind was so great we could not keep to our course. Happily for us we came upon some timber near Las Vegas, in which we were able to take refuge. We had one man frozen to death and I subsequently learned that many of the Indians we had been pursuing perished in the same storm. After it was over, we went on to Las Vegas, then in command of Captain Judd.[118] From there the command marched to Taos, and I proceeded to Rayado, where I remained until the spring of 1850.

A detachment of ten dragoons, commanded by Leigh Holbrook, was stationed at Rayado during the winter. Sometime in March a party of Indians attacked the rancho where our animals were grazing, about two miles distant from where we were living. Two men were in charge of it, and both were severely wounded. One of them made his way in to Rayado, however, and gave the alarm. The dragoons, three Americans, and myself immediately saddled up

[118] Captain Henry B. Judd of the Third U. S. Artillery, graduate from West Point in the class of 1839 and on frontier duty at Santa Fé, Taos, and Las Vegas from 1848 to 1850.

and proceeded to the rancho. It was night when we arrived, and we remained until morning, when we took the trail of the animals that had been stolen. We followed it at a gallop for twenty-five miles, when we discovered the Indians at a distance. During the pursuit some of our animals gave out and were left on the trail.

We approached the Indians cautiously, and when we were close enough, we charged them. We killed five, and the other four made their escape. We recovered all but four of the stolen animals.[119] Two of the men with me on this enterprise have since been slain by the same tribe of Indians; Sergeant Holbrook, a brave and gallant soldier, was killed in the battle of Ceneguilla in 1854, and William New, a brave and experienced trapper, was killed at Rayado a few months after our pursuit of the Indians that had stolen our horses.[120]

[119] Sergeant Holbrook's report of this affair is printed in Sabin, *Kit Carson Days*, 351-52. The five Indians killed were scalped, the scalps being retained as a "voucher" according to the gallant sergeant. In transmitting this report to his superiors at Washington, Major Grier thought it desirable to explain that the scalps were taken "by two or three Mexican herders who came up after the fight was over."

[120] New was surprised and surrounded while working his farm. Although he had his rifle it was empty, but

Kit Carson's Autobiography

On May 5, 1850, Tim Goodel and I started to Fort Laramie with forty or fifty head of mules and horses to trade with the emigrants. We arrived about the first of June and remained about a month, disposing of our animals to good advantage. Goodel then started to California, while I set out for home. At the Greenhorn River, a tributary of the Arkansas, I learned that the Apaches were watching the road ahead of me to waylay and murder any travelers who came along. I remained here about six days to recruit my animals. My only companion was a Mexican boy, and I could get only one other man, Charles Kinney, to accompany me.

I set out, and traveled about forty miles through the mountains the first night, to the Trinchera River. Here I had the animals concealed in the brush, at some distance from the road, while I climbed the highest cottonwood tree to watch for Indians. I remained in this look-out all day. At times I would drop asleep and nearly fall from my perch, but would recover in time and continue my watch. Towards evening I saw a

by pretending the contrary, he kept his assailants at bay for a time. When they finally rushed him, he put up a desperate fight with clubbed rifle, before finally succumbing to his wounds. See Peters, *Life and Adventures of Kit Carson*, 349–50.

large body of Indians about half a mile distant. They had not as yet discovered our trail. I descended the tree, and we saddled up and proceeded on our journey, keeping in the brush some distance off the road until dark. We then took to the road and reached Red River at daylight, and Taos that evening.

I remained at Taos a few days and then departed for Rayado. During my absence, the Indians had run off every head of livestock. The troops were stationed there at the time, but the Indians came in such force that they feared to attack them. Shortly afterwards, a detachment of soldiers commanded by Major Grier was sent in pursuit of them. They killed some of the Indians, and recovered all the livestock except that which had been killed by the Indians.

I remained at Rayado till fall [1850]. Nothing of any moment transpired, except my pursuit of an American who had organized a party for the purpose of murdering Mr. Samuel Weatherhead and Mr. Elias Brevoort, on the plains. The two men were supposed to have a large amount of money. The object of the party was disclosed by Fox to a man in Taos, whom he was seeking to induce to join him. The man declined to do so, and when he thought Fox had gone too far to be apprehended, he revealed what he had told him.

Lieutenant Taylor of the First Dragoons[121] was in Taos at the time. He told me that he wished Fox apprehended for debt, and requested me to pursue him for this purpose. I refused to do so, whereupon he stated the true reason for wishing him apprehended, which was that Fox and a party of men were traveling in company with Mr. Weatherhead and Brevoort, intending to murder them as soon as they reached the Cimarron, and then go to Texas. As soon as I learned of this plot I agreed to go, and ten dragoons were given to me as an escort. On the second night out we traveled until one o'clock, when we met Captain Ewell[122] in command of a party of recruits en route for New Mexico. I told him the object of my journey, and he joined me with twenty-five men.

On reaching the camp of Weatherhead and Brevoort, we entered it cautiously and

[121] Oliver H. P. Taylor was graduated from West Point in 1846 and appointed to the First U. S. Dragoons. He served in the Mexican War, and for several years thereafter was stationed in the Southwest. He was slain in battle on the Spokane expedition, May 17, 1858. He was but twenty-five years old in 1850, and his attempted subterfuge with Carson may perhaps be accounted for by his youth and inexperience.

[122] Captain Richard S. Ewell, a graduate from West Point in 1840. A Virginian, he joined the Confederacy in the Civil War, and attained the rank of lieutenant general.

arrested Fox. The next day Captain Ewell returned to his camp with Fox in his custody. Weatherhead and Brevoort retained fifteen of their men, in whom they had confidence, and ordered the remainder, about thirty-five in number, to leave them. I have not the least doubt that they would have been murdered if these men had not been expelled from their party. They told me that anything I might ask of them would be freely given, but I demanded nothing for my trouble, deeming it sufficient reward to have saved the lives of two valuable citizens. However, in the spring following, they made me accept a splendid pair of silver-mounted pistols as a present.

I returned to Rayado with Fox, and turned him over to the proper authorities. He was taken to Taos and confined there, but nothing positive could be proved against him, and he was liberated.

I remained in Rayado till March, 1851, and then started for St. Louis, taking twelve wagons belonging to Mr. Maxwell with me for the purpose of bringing back goods for him. I arrived at the Kansas River on May 1, and proceeding to St. Louis, purchased the goods. I then returned to the Kansas, where I loaded the wagons and started for home. I concluded to take the Bent's Fort trail on account of water and grass being in greater abundance thereon.

About fifteen miles before reaching the crossing of the Arkansas, I fell in with a village of Cheyenne Indians. They were hostile to the United States at this time, because one of the officers of Colonel Summer's command (which was about ten days' march ahead of me) had flogged a Chief of their tribe. I do not know the reason for this punishment, but I presume courage was oozing from the finger tips of the officer, and finding the Indians in his power, he wished to be relieved of their presence. An Indian very seldom lets an injury go unavenged, and it is immaterial who his victim may be, so long as he belongs to the same nation as the offender. Unfortunately, I happened to be the first American to pass them since the insult was given, and on me they proposed to retaliate.

I was encamped about twenty miles from their village when they began coming in in groups of one, two, and three, until twenty had arrived. At first I thought they were friendly, not having heard of the outrage that had been inflicted on them. I treated them with kindness, and invited them to sit down and smoke and talk. They did so, but soon they commenced talking among themselves and I understood them to say that they could easily kill me with a knife while I was smoking and off my guard, while, as for the Mexicans with me, they could slay them as easily as if they were buffalo.

I was alarmed by this talk, for I had but fifteen men with me, two Americans and thirteen Mexicans, and I had but a poor opinion of the bravery of the latter. I told the Indians that I was ignorant of the cause of their wishing my scalp, and that I had done them no injury and had wanted to treat them kindly; they had come to me as friends, but I now discovered that they wished to kill me and they must leave my camp; any who refused would be shot, and if they attempted to return I would fire on them. They departed, and joined the rest of the band, who were in sight on the hills. I then ordered my men to hitch up, and we moved on, the drivers carrying their rifles in one hand, and their whips in the other. We traveled in this way until dark, when we encamped and I started an express to Rayado.

On the following day, we had stopped at noon, when five Indians approached us. When they came within 100 yards of us, I ordered them to halt, but eventually I let them come in, so that I could speak more freely to them. I informed them that I had sent an express to Rayado the night before to bring the troops who were stationed there; that I had many friends among them, and they would surely come to my relief. If I were killed, they would know by whom it was done, and my death would be avenged.

They left me and examined the road, finding that all I said was true, and that the express had advanced so far that they could not overtake him. Fearing the arrival of the troops, they concluded to leave me. I am confident that my party would have been killed by the Cheyennes (for there were a large number around me) if I had not sent ahead for assistance, and I afterwards learned that the only reason they had for attacking me was the resentment caused by the conduct of the officer of Colonel Summer's command.

My express reached Colonel Summer on the third day after he left me, and gave him the letter he bore, but as Colonel Summer[123] would send me no aid, the express continued on and arrived at Rayado the next day and gave my letter to Major Grier, who immediately detailed Lieutenant Johnston and a party of men to march to my relief. When Lieutenant Johnston met Colonel Summer,

[123] Apparently Colonel Edwin V. Sumner, who served with distinction in the Mexican and the Civil Wars, and who was governor of New Mexico from 1851 to 1853.

he was asked where he was going, and when he replied, to my assistance, I presume the conscience of the gallant old Colonel troubled him. He had refused to send help to aid me two days before, and supposed that in all probability my party and I had been murdered. Everyone knew that if Johnston, who was a brave and noble officer, should have a fight with the Indians, the affair would be properly managed and he would receive great praise. So the Colonel wished to have a hand in the matter, and concluded to send Major Carleton and thirty men with Johnston. I do not consider myself under any obligation to him, for by his conduct two days earlier he showed plainly that he had no desire to render aid to a few American citizens who were in the power of a band of Indians, who had been enraged by the conduct of some of his own command.

But I am thankful to Major Carleton and Lieutenant Johnston for the kindness they showed me on their arrival at my camp, and for their anxiety and their willingness to punish the Indians who had sought to interrupt me. Major Grier, a gentleman and a gallant soldier, is also entitled to my warmest gratitude for his promptness in sending assistance to me and for the cordial way he met the responsibility to which he had been appointed. It plainly showed that he had a noble heart and that he can be depended upon in the hour of danger.

The services of the troops were not required, for the Indians knew they would come, and before their arrival they had removed beyond striking distance. The troops met me about twenty-five miles from Bent's Fort, and I returned with them to Rayado. I delivered the wagons and goods to Mr. Maxwell and remained here until March, 1852.

Mr. Maxwell and I now rigged up a party of eighteen men to go trapping, I taking charge of them. We went to the Balla Salado, and down the South Fork to the plains; through the plains of Laramie River to the New Park, trapped it to the Old Park, trapped it again, then again to the Balla Salado, then on to the Arkansas where it comes out of the mountain; we then followed it on under the mountain, thence home to the Rayado, through the Raton Mountains, having made a very good hunt.[124]

I remained at Rayado during the fall and winter. In February, 1853, I went to the Rio

[124] This trapping expedition, described by Carson in a single paragraph, lasted several months. For it, Carson had assembled eighteen of his former cronies for an expedition which was intended as a final farewell to their life as mountain men.

Abajo Valley and purchased a flock of 6,500 sheep. I returned with them to Rayado, and then I started for California with them. Henry Mercure and John Bernavette and their employees accompanied me. We first went to Fort Laramie, and then kept to the wagon road that is traveled by emigrants to California. We arrived about the first of August, having met with no serious loss. We did very well with our sheep, selling them to Mr. Norris at $5.50 a head.[125]

Hearing so much talk of the great change that had taken place at San Francisco, I concluded to go there. When I arrived, I would not have known the place if I had not been there so often before.[126]

Maxwell came on to California shortly afterwards, and disposed of his sheep in Sacramento. From Carson River he sent an express on to me, which I received at Sacramento, requesting me to await his arrival so that we could travel home together by way

[125] In New Mexico the sheep had cost a few cents each. Carson's exploit in driving them in safety to California is not the least of his achievements.

[126] Half a dozen years earlier, when Carson knew the place, it was a sleepy Spanish town of perhaps two hundred inhabitants. In the interval it had grown to a bustling city of almost forty thousand. Dr. Peters relates that the Californians lionized Carson, which proved so distasteful to him that he cut short his visit.

of the Gila. When he arrived, I went down
to Los Angeles by land, while he took the
steamer. I would not travel by sea, having
made a voyage in 1846 with which I was so disgusted that I swore it would be the last time
I would ever lose sight of land while I could
get a mule to carry me. Maxwell reached Los
Angeles about fifteen days ahead of me. We
made the necessary preparations for our
journey and then set out for New Mexico.

We soon arrived at the village of the Pima
Indians. From here, on account of the
scarcity of grass, we continued up the Gila
to the mouth of the San Pedro. We ascended
this stream for three days and then took a
straight course for the copper mines. From
here we went on to the River Del Norte, and
thence home through the settlements of the
Rio Abajo, arriving at Taos on December
25, 1853.

On my way home, I saw the Mormon
delegate to Congress and was informed by
him that I had received the appointment of
Indian agent, and on my arrival at Taos, I
accepted it and gave the necessary bond.[127]

[127] The acceptance of this appointment as Indian agent
marks the beginning of a new period in Carson's career.
Save for his illiteracy, which proved a source of trouble
in keeping his accounts, he was almost ideally qualified
for his new work.

Kit Carson's Autobiography

In February, 1854, the Jicarilla Apaches showed a hostile disposition. Lieutenant Beall of the Second Dragoons had a fight with them on the waters of Red River, in which one or two soldiers were killed and several wounded, but he killed a number of the Indians and forced them to retreat. He charged them once or twice, and although they were superior in numbers, they could not maintain their ground.

In March, I proceeded to Santa Fé on business pertaining to my office. Shortly before my departure a large party of Jicarilla Apaches came within twenty miles of Taos. I saw a number of the chiefs and they all pretended friendship, but during my absence they became hostile. Lieutenant J. W. Davidson of the First Dragoons and sixty dragoons of Companies F and I were ordered out against them, and overtook them in the Embudo Mountains, about twenty miles southwest of Taos. Judging from the preparations they had made and from their having chosen such an advantageous position, the Indians evidently intended to fight the troops sent against them, unless they should come in force.

Lieutenant Davidson had sixty men and there were seventy-five or eighty lodges of Indians. When he advanced upon them, they immediately perceived his numbers and came to the conclusion to fight, for when a few men were sent in advance, they did not speak to them in a friendly manner, but instead made hostile demonstrations, and Lieutenant Davidson was compelled to attack them. I know him well, having been in engagements where he played a prominent part, and I know him to be as brave as an officer can be.[128] I have been told by the men who were in the engagement that day that he never once took ambush during the fight, and that when he was forced to retreat, he directed his men to take shelter as best they could while he, fearless of danger, remained exposed to the fire of the Indians.

The Indians were in position on the side and top of the mountain, and the troops occupied the bank of a small stream below. The Indians could not be reached on horseback, and the dragoons had to fight on foot, leaving a few men to guard their horses. They ascended the mountain and drove the Indians from their position, but lost five men in doing so. The Indians were in great force, and had the troops surrounded; they

---

[128] Lieutenant Davidson had been with Kearny's Army of the West, to which Carson had been unceremoniously attached by that leader in the summer of 1846.

made an attempt to secure the horses, but through the timely arrival of Lieutenant Davidson they failed. They kept up a fire on the troops from every direction. Meanwhile, they could not be seen by the soldiers, as they were concealed behind trees and in the brush.

The troops charged them several times, but the Indians whom they dislodged merely retreated and joined those in the rear. Finding that it was impossible to do any execution on account of the situation in which he was placed, and having lost several men in killed and wounded, Lieutenant Davidson was finally compelled reluctantly to retreat. The officer who was with him, seeing the deplorable condition of his men, persuaded him to give up the idea of maintaining his position. The retreat was sounded, and the Indians in great numbers pursued the troops, who had to wheel about several times and charge them. They finally succeeded in reaching the main road to Taos, but with a loss of twenty-two soldiers killed and nearly every one of the command wounded. The number of Indians who fell has never been ascertained, but there is no doubt that many of them were slain. I returned to Taos the day after the fight, passing close to the battle-field, but I did not meet a single

Indian.[129] They had all fled across the Del Norte.

Lieutenant-Colonel Cooke of the Second Dragoons promptly organized a force to pursue and chastise the Indians. He employed a company of forty Pueblo Indians and Mexicans under the command of Mr. James H. Quinn as captain and John Martin as his lieutenant. They were well qualified for the duty assigned them, which was to act as spies, proceeding in advance of the main body and keeping the trail of the Indians. I accompanied them, serving as principal guide to the expedition.

The march was begun on April 4, 1854. We advanced to the Arroyo Hondo, some ten miles north of Taos, and then moved down this stream to its junction with the Rio Grande, passing through a deep cañon which was difficult for troops to traverse. The Rio Del Norte was high at that time, but it had to be crossed. The bed of the river is full of large rocks, and in crossing the horses would sometimes be in water only

[129] This was the battle of Cieneguilla, fought March 30, 1854. Lieutenant Davidson had graduated from West Point in 1845, and until the Civil War served chiefly on the southwestern frontier. He served with distinction in the Civil War, being brevetted major general for gallant and meritorious service in the field.

knee-deep, and then would have to step off a ledge into water over their backs, and would find difficulty in ascending the next rock.

I took the lead and finally got across. The troops then commenced their passage, meeting with no very serious accident, save for two or three of the dragoons, who came near being drowned. The dragoon horses had to be sent back to be used in crossing the infantry. I crossed and recrossed the river about twenty times[130] before the task was finished, and the entire command was assembled on the other bank.

We had now to ascend from the river. The cañon is 600 feet high at the lowest calculation, but by leading the animals cautiously through the different windings of the trail we at length ascended it, and continued our march over a plain in which there were many cañons and deep ravines, entirely destitute of both water and grass. We finally arrived at a small Mexican town named Servilleta, where we encamped and where forage was purchased for the animals. In the morning we resumed our march. We were two days finding the trail, and we followed it for two days more before we overtook the Indians.

[130] Being each time immersed, of course, in the icy water of the river, swollen by the melting mountain snow.

They saw us approaching and retreated. We pursued them, killing several Indians and capturing their camp equipage and a number of horses. We had one soldier killed, and one wounded.

Captain Sykes, who was in command of the infantry, deserves great praise for his conduct on this march. Although he had a horse with him, I do not think he mounted it once during the entire campaign. He waded the streams and trudged through the ice and snow, often for as much as ten miles, and I really believe that it was by reason of his conduct that his men maintained their courage. I cannot understand how they were able to undergo such hardships. The marches were long, over high mountains covered with snow, and owing to the deficiency of means of transporting the baggage, the troops were commonly on half rations. They surely would have broken down from fatigue and the want of provisions if they had not had a leader who was always in the advance, and who willingly endured the same hardships they had to undergo.

When the Indians were first sighted, Captain Sykes was leading the advance with his company, the spies being some distance ahead of him. When they were told that the Indians were ahead, he and his men charged forward on the run, and entered the Indian village alongside the dragoons. The soldier who was killed, and the one who was wounded, both belonged to his company. We pursued the Indians through a deep cañon for about four miles. Many of them we did not even see, but seven were killed and a number wounded. When darkness fell, the command returned to the Indian camp and bivouacked for the night.

In the morning the wounded man was sent back, under the escort of a corporal and a squad of soldiers, to receive medical aid. The remainder of the command took the trail of the Indians, following them through deep cañons and over lofty mountains covered with snow, but they could not again be overtaken. They broke up into small bands and their trails led in different directions. If one of them were followed, at night the pursuers would find they had returned almost to the same place from which they had started in the morning. The Jicarilla Apaches are the most difficult of all Indians to pursue. After an attack, they always retreat in small parties. Having no baggage, they are able to travel several days without food, and it is impossible for any body of regular troops to overtake them. We followed them six days, when the commanding officer, finding that they could not be overtaken, concluded to march to Abiquiu, a Mexican village situated on the Rio Chama (a tributary of the Del Norte) for the purpose of recruiting his animals. He arrived there about the fourteenth of April.

The party that had returned with the wounded man encountered a Utah Indian, whom they took prisoner, and deprived of his arms and horse. He presently made his escape and rejoined his tribe. Colonel Cooke was afraid that such treatment given a friendly Indian might cause his tribe to join the Indians who were at war with us. I immediately set out for my agency at Taos, having first sent a man to the Utah village to inform the headmen that I wanted to talk to them, and to request them to come in to the Agency to see me. In a short time after my arrival, several came. I told them that the soldiers who had captured one of their tribe had done so thinking that he was an Apache; that the Americans did not wish to do them any injury, and that I hoped they would remain friendly and not render any aid to the Indians who were at war with us. If they did so, they would be treated as enemies. They promised not to render any assistance to the Apaches. I then returned the property our men had captured, and they departed, while I remained at the Agency.

After remaining a few days at Abiquiu, Colonel Cooke marched in pursuit of the hostile Indians. He followed them several days, when he was caught in a snow storm, and the trail being many days old and the ground covered with snow, it was useless to proceed farther. He then returned to the Rio Colorado, where he was joined by a reinforcement of troops under command of Major Brooks of the Third Infantry.

As soon as the necessary preparations could be made, another campaign was to be made against the enemy. Colonel Cooke took command of the troops that had been engaged in the two preceding campaigns and marched to Taos. The men were much worn down by the hardships they had undergone and the animals were badly used up, and both men and horses required repose. I can say of Colonel Cooke that he is as efficient an Indian fighter as I have ever accompanied; that he is brave and gallant everyone knows. By reason of his persevering pursuit of them, the Indians lost many of their number from hardships and the severe cold, and they would not have been able to elude him, if they had not been so fortunate as to have kept the horses they had captured in their fight with Lieutenant Davidson, but would have been caught and chastised so thoroughly that war with that tribe would never have occurred again.

Major Brooks now took the field against the Indians, and after following their trail for several days, he arrived in the Utah country. Finding that the country was entirely cut up with trails and that it was impossible to identify the one made by the enemy, he was compelled to give up the pursuit and return to Taos, where he arrived about the fifteenth of May. He had been in the field some ten or fifteen days and had not encountered a single enemy.

Major Carleton of the First Dragoons was encamped in Taos, making preparations for a campaign. By the twenty-third of May he was ready to march. I accompanied him as principal guide. We marched north to Fort Massachusetts, where the spies under command of Captain Quinn turned west to the White Mountains and thence along their base to the Mosco Pass, and through this to the Huerfano, his object being to discover the trail. From the place where Major Brooks gave up the pursuit, it was evident that the Indians were making for the Mosco Pass. The command marched through the Sangre de Cristo Pass, Major Carleton having agreed to join Captain Quinn on the Huerfano in three days. I discovered the trail of three Indians in the Pass, and followed it till I came to the main trail near the Huerfano. At the entrance of the Mosco Pass Captain Quinn discovered an old encampment of the Indians. As we had anticipated, they had gone through the Pass. We now followed the main trail for six days through very rugged country. Mountains, cañons, and ravines had to be passed, but at last we overtook the Indians, encamped in the Raton Mountains on the east side of Fisher's Peak.

The troops charged their village, and the Indians fled. Some of them were killed and about forty of their horses were captured. The soldiers followed them until it became dark. A party of men under command of Lieutenant R. Johnston of the First Dragoons and Captain Quinn and three of his spies, were left behind at the village. They concealed themselves in the brush, and one of the spies who knew the rallying call made by these Indians when they were scattered, sounded it. Two warriors and two squaws made their appearance. The spies fired on them and killed one of the warriors. The noise of the firing and the yells of those who escaped warned the Indians of the proximity of the soldiers, and nothing more was accomplished. The brush was thick in the vicinity of the village, and afforded many hiding places in which the Indians took refuge.

It was entirely owing to the good management of Major Carleton that the Indians were discovered. He directed the spies to keep the trail, and the troops followed them, keeping concealed as much as possible by marching through the brush and timber. In the morning of the day we overtook the Indians, I saw a trail that was fresh, and told the Major that if we met with no accident we would find them by two o'clock. He replied that if this proved to be the case, he would give me one of the finest hats that could be procured in New York. The Indians were found at the very hour I had predicted, and the Major fulfilled his promise, presenting me a hat which he had made in New York—and a fine one it was.

The command now marched back for a few miles and encamped for the night. Next day we began the return journey to Taos, traveling to the headwaters of the Canadian and its tributaries. We passed through a beautiful mountain country and arrived at Taos in June. I did not engage in any other campaign for the remainder of the year.

In July, Major Blake of the First Dragoons made another campaign. He was absent some time, but did not find any Indians. In August, I left the Agency to visit the Utahs for the purpose of collecting them to meet the Superintendent at Abiquiu in October. To accomplish this, I had to travel about two hundred miles, and pass close to a village of Apaches. I got by without being discovered by them and arrived at the Utah village. I told the natives that the Superintendent wished to see them in October, and they agreed to pay him a visit. I then set out for the Agency, arriving home a few days later.

In October I proceeded to the Council. The Indians attended as they had promised to do. Presents were given to them, and they appeared friendly. Shortly previous to the Council, however, some Mexicans had killed a Utah for the purpose of stealing his coat. The Indians were much dissatisfied, requesting payment in horses for the death of the Indian. This was refused them, but they were promised that the murderers would be arrested and punished according to law. One of the murderers was apprehended eventually, but he made his escape soon after, and no further efforts were made to render justice to the Indians.

The smallpox broke out among the Indians while they were on their way to their hunting grounds, and the leading men of the band of Muache Utahs died. They now came to the conclusion that the Superintendent was the cause of this affliction, and that he had collected them for the purpose of injuring them. He had given a blanket coat to each of the headmen, and since everyone who received a coat had died, the Indians firmly believed that the coats were the cause of the deaths. Aside from this, the murderer of the Indians had been allowed to go unpunished, and the Indians had but little faith in anything the Superintendent promised them, so they prepared for war, and joining the Apaches, commenced their depredations. They attacked the settlement of Costilla, drove off nearly all the stock, and stole and murdered all the citizens they could find.

The regular troops in the country were not strong enough to take the field against the Utahs and the Apaches combined, and the Governor issued a proclamation calling for six companies of volunteers. The response was immediate and the companies were organized. Several more companies than there was need for offered their services, showing the willingness of the people to perform military service when called upon to punish their enemies. If the chastisement of the Indians of this country were left to the citizens, I have no doubt but that in a short period they would subdue them. As matters stand at present, the Indians are the masters of the country, and commit depredations whenever they please. Perhaps a command of troops is sent after them; they are overtaken, and some of the property they stole is recovered, while they make their escape unpunished. The Superintendent then calls them in to have a grand talk. Presents are given and promises are made, but only to be broken when it becomes convenient to break them. As long as these mountain Indians are permitted to run at large this country will always remain in its impoverished state, and the only remedy is to compel them to live in settlements, cultivate the soil, and learn to gain their maintenance independently of the general government.

After the organization of the volunteers, the Governor appointed Captain Ceran St. Vrain of Taos as their commander. He was a gentleman in every manner qualified for this office, having passed the greater part of his life in the mountains and in this Territory. When the people learned of the appointment there was great rejoicing, for all knew that the Captain was a gentleman and the bravest of soldiers, and they were confident that under his leadership the Indians would be punished so thoroughly that it would be long before they would again commence hostilities. In fact, this was the only appointment of the Governor that met the approbation of the people, and many were surprised at his sound judgment in making such a noble choice.

In February, 1855, Colonel T. T. Fauntleroy of the First Dragoons arrived in Taos and began preparing to take the field. He had under his command four companies of volunteers commanded by Colonel St. Vrain, two companies of dragoons, one of artillery, and one of spies. The latter was commanded by Lucien Stewart of this place, a gentleman who has passed a great deal of his life in the mountains, and having had a great deal of experience in Indian warfare, he was well qualified to perform the duties for which he was employed.

The command left Taos early in March, and traveled north to Fort Massachusetts; from here it marched to the Rio Del Norte, up this river to the place it leaves the mountain, and thence north to the Saquachi Pass, where the Indians were found in force. They were attacked, and defeated, losing a number of warriors killed and wounded. After the fight the artillery company was left at the Saquachi Pass in charge of the train of provisions. It was a very important position, requiring an officer who was judicious and fearless of danger. Lieutenant Lloyd Beall of the Second Artillery was chosen for this duty, which he discharged to the satisfaction of the Colonel.

The main command continued in pursuit of the Indians and after a few days discovered a large party on the headwaters of the Arkansas. The soldiers charged upon them immediately and defeated them. Some of the warriors were killed, and many horses were taken. We then began the return march, traversing the Mosco Pass and reaching Fort Massachusetts at the end of March. The country we passed through while en route to Saquachi Pass was level and covered with snow, and during this time the weather was as cold as I have ever experienced. The remainder of the march was over high mountains covered with snow.

I returned to Taos, while the command was distributed among the several settlements so that forage could be procured for the animals, which were in a very reduced condition. The soldiers remained at the settlements until the middle of April, and then started on another campaign. I did not accompany this expedition. Colonel T. T. Fauntleroy took the same direction as the one followed in the previous campaign, and traveled to the Punchi Pass,[131] where the Indians were found and entirely routed. Many of them were killed, and a number of animals and much camp equipage were captured. Colonel St. Vrain now marched through the Sangre de Cristo Pass and on to the Purgatoire River, where the Indians were discovered. They were completely routed, and their animals and baggage captured. He then followed their trail, sending out men in pursuit of them in every direction. Warriors were killed daily, and their women taken prisoners. In this campaign the Apaches received a chastisement for their many depredations, such as they had thought could never be given them.

The command now returned to Taos, and Colonel Fauntleroy did not again take the field. The volunteers had but a short period to serve, but St. Vrain did not allow them to be idle. He immediately took the field again, and kept them in pursuit of the Indians until a few days before the expiration of their time of service. If they had continued in the service three months longer and had been under

[131] Near present-day Salida, Colorado.

the command and sole direction of Colonel St. Vrain, there would never again have been any need of troops in this part of the country. The Indians would have been entirely subjected, and in all probability but a few of them would have remained to cause trouble in the future. But this was not to be. The authorities in control considered the Indians had been sufficiently punished; and when they asked for peace, it was granted them.

In August the Superintendent made treaties with the Indians that had not been at war. In September the hostile Indians came in and received presents, and promised friendship for the future. Not all of the Apaches came in at the time of the treaty, however. Some of them remained out committing depredations, and this fact was reported to the Superintendent, but he would not believe it. No treaty should have been made with the Apaches, for no faith can be placed in their promises.

By the treaties that were made, the Indians were promised certain sums yearly in case they wished to settle on some stream and commence farming, and they were given their choice of country to settle. The Superintendent went on to Washington with his treaties, which were laid before the Senate. They have not been confirmed as yet, nor should they be, as they are not of a character to suit the people. The Apaches are now committing depredations daily, which go unpunished, and in my opinion they may again commence hostilities ere long. The other tribes with whom treaties were made will comply with their provisions, I think, and will not be hostile again if the Government does not stop their supplies of provisions during such times as they cannot hunt.

I frequently visit the Indians, speak to them of the advantages of peace, and exert my influence to keep them satisfied with the proceedings of those placed in power over them. On September fourth, 1856, I attended the assembly of Indians held by the Superintendent at Abiquiu for the purpose of giving them presents. They appeared to be contented, but there was a disturbance the next day. A Tabaguachi Utah had been given a blanket which was old and worn. He was dissatisfied, and tore it up, and endeavored to kill the Superintendent, but was prevented by the other Indians.

I cannot see how the Superintendent can expect any of the Indians to depart satisfied after he has called them to see him from a distance of two or three hundred miles, and compelled them to go several days without anything to eat, except what they have brought with them. They are given a meal by the Superintendent, after which the presents are distributed. Some receive a blanket; those that get none are given a knife, or a hatchet, or some vermillion, or a piece of red or blue cloth, or some sugar, and perhaps a few more trinkets. If they were left in their own country, they could more than earn the quantity of gifts they receive in one day's hunt. They could hunt for skins and furs, and the traders could furnish them with the same articles which the Government gives them, and they would be saved the necessity of coming such a distance, with the consequent fatigue to their animals, and the necessity of having to travel without food themselves. If presents are given, it should be done in their own country. They should not be allowed to come into the settlements, for every visit an Indian makes to a town causes him more or less injury.

I am now living in Taos, N. M., in the discharge of my official duties as an Indian agent. I am daily visited by the Indians, and I give them presents, as directed by the Superintendent. I am opposed to the policy of having Indians come to the settlements, but as no agency buildings are allowed to be built in the Indian country, necessity compels them to come to the towns.

The foregoing I hereby transfer to Mr. Jesse B. Turly to be used as he may deem proper for our Joint Benefit.

C. CARSON

Index

Index

Index

Beall, Col. Benjamin L., career, 127; conducts Indian campaigns, 127–29.

Beall, Lieut. Lloyd, defeats Apache, 149; commands Saquachi Pass, 165.

Bear River (Calif.), Frémont camps near, 105.

Bear River (Utah), trappers visit, 23; Frémont ascends, 77.

Beaubien, Charles (Carlos), recipient of Maxwell Land Grant, 130.

Beaver, hunted, 11, 14, 39, 45; sold, 16, 21, 33, 59, 62; stolen, 28; scarcity, 63.

Beckwourth, James, employed by Louis Vasquez, 55.

Benevides, Carmel, marries Antoine Robidoux, 35.

Bent, Charles, career, 33–34; kindness, 64; slain, 65; aids Carson, xi, 71.

Bent, George, reports Carson-Shunar duel, 44.

Bent, William, career, 33–34.

Benton, Mrs. Thomas H., conversation with Carson, 44.

Benton, Senator Thomas H., advertises Frémont, xii; entertains Carson, 68, 119–20; geographical error, 78; message to Frémont, 99.

Bent's Fort (Fort William), trappers visit, 63–64; Carson visits, 68, 71, 73, 87–88; route via, 141.

Bent's Fort on South Fork of Platte, see Fort St. Vrain.

Bernavette, John, as companion of Carson, 147.

Bidwell, John, narrative cited, 22, 35, 46, 53, 81.

Big Horn River, trappers visit, 45–46; relation to Wind River, 56.

Big Snake River, see Snake River.

Bijoux River, route via, 125.

Blackfoot Indians, warfare with trappers, 22, 39–42, 47, 50–52, 56–58, 60–62; smallpox ravages, 48.

Black Hills, trappers visit, 55.

Blackwell, ——, leads trappers, 29.

Black Whiteman, describes Indian fight, 28.

Blake, Major ——, leads Indian campaign, 161.

"Bloody Kansas," Bill Mitchell's experience, 63–64.

174

Index

Bloom, Prof. Lansing, B., aid acknowledged, xxxii.

Bonneville, Capt. Benjamin L. E., maps Great Basin, 78.

Boone, Daniel, popularity, ix–x.

Boone's Lick Country, Carsons migrate to, 3.

Brevoort, Elias, Carson rescues, 139–41.

Brewerton, Lieut. George D., narrative cited, xxix–xxxi, 35; as companion of Carson, 123–24.

Bridger, James, mode of speech, xxviii; career, 37; attends trappers' rendezvous, 39, 62; pursues Indians, 42; builds Fort Bridger, 55; leads trappers, 57; Carson joins, 59.

Broadus, Andrew, leg amputated, 5–6.

Brooks, Major ——, leads Indian campaign, 157–58.

Brown's Hole, identified, 54; Carson winters at, 62; Frémont visits, 87. See also Fort Robidoux.

Buchanan, James, message to Frémont, 99.

Buena Ventura River, mythical idea of, 78.

Buffalo, Carson hunts, 47; menace trappers, 49.

Burgess, ——, captured, 115.

CACHE, of beaver, made, 28.

Cache-la-poudre, route via, 75.

California, expedition of Ewing Young, 7, 10–22; missions, 13–16; Spanish Trail to, 35, 82, 86, 123; Capt. Joseph Walker visits, 45; emigrant route to, 67; Frémont visits, 78–82, 91–119; news of war with Mexico received, 96; of gold discovery, 123; Americans conquer, 105–22; estate of Frémont in, 126–27; sheep driven to, 147–48.

Camp, Charles L., connection with Carson autobiography, xvi–xviii; aid acknowledged, xxxii; article cited, xvi, 11, 95, 106.

Campbell, Robert, builder of Fort Laramie, 49.

Campbell, Prof. W. S., see Stanley Vestal.

Canadian, slain, 86.

Cañon, Grand, mentioned, 12.

Index

Carleton, Major James H., rescues Carson, 145; leads Indian campaign, 158–60.

Carson, Christopher (Kit), popularity, ix–x, career, xi–xii, 3–5; fame, xii–xiii, 135; autobiography written xi,xiii–xxvii; characterized, xxvii–xxxiv; mode of speech, xxvii–xxviii; modesty, xxix–xxxi; crosses plains, 5–6; visits Taos, 9, 33, 71–72, 87, 127–28, 139, 148, 151, 165; Chihuahua sojourn, 8–9; member of Ewing Young's expedition, 9–22; leads trappers, 18–19; joins Fitzpatrick, 22, 37; joins Capt. Gaunt, 23–24; fights Indians, 24–28, 30–32, 40–42, 50–52, 60–62, 72–73, 96–104, 121–22, 131–35, 152–65; pursues deserters, 28–29; member of Capt. Lee's party, 33–37; marries, 34, 68–69; kills horse-thief, 36–37; adventure with grizzlies, 38; duel with Shunar, 42–44; joins Hudson's Bay Company outfit, 45; visits Fort Hall, 46–47, 59, 75; member of Fontanelle's party, 47–53; of Thompson and St. Clair's party, 54; of James Bridger's party, 55, 59; of Northwest Fur Company party, 59; as hunter at Fort Davy Crockett, 54–55; winters at Brown's Hole, 62; abandons trapping, 63; as employee of Bent and St. Vrain, 64; visits St. Louis, 65, 119, 125, 141; guides Frémont, 65–68, 73–108; guides Gen. Kearny, 109; carries despatches, 71–72, 108–109, 115–17, 119–26; aids Mexicans, 82–85; establishes home, 87–88, 130; kills Mexicans, 106; in battle of San Pasqual, 110–13; tribute to Frémont, 126–27; expedition to Fort Laramie, 138–39; to St. Louis, 141–46; farewell trapping expedition, 146; sheep speculation, 147–48; services as Indian agent, 148–49, 156–57, 168–70.

Carson, Lindsay, father of Kit Carson, career, 3.

Carson, Moses, brother of Kit Carson, 3.

Carson River, Frémont ascends, 91; Maxwell visits, 147.

Castle Island, see Disappointment Island.

Index

Castro, Gen. José, hostilities with Frémont, 93–94, 105–106.

Cheyenne Indians, tradition of battle cited, 28; William Bent marries, 34; relations of George Bent with, 44; encounter of Carson with, 142–46.

Cieneguilla, battle of, 137, 149–52.

Clark, Arthur H., owner of Carson autobiography, xv–xvi.

Clarke, S. A., history cited, 8.

Clear Creek, trading post of Louis Vasquez on, 54.

Coan, Charles F., history cited, 130.

Coast Range, explorers view, 79; cross, 82.

Colfax County (N. Mex.), site of Maxwell Land Grant, 130.

Colorado River, Ewing Young's party visits, 9, 12–13, 19; army visits, 157.

Columbia River, objective of Ogden party, 15; of Frémont, 95; Frémont descends, 77.

Comanche Indians, Bill Mitchell joins tribe, 63; warfare with whites, 120–21, 124.

Congress, naval vessel, 117.

Connelley, Wm. E., edits journal of Cooke expedition, 69.

Cooke, Capt. Philip St. George, career, 69; protects Mexicans, 69–70; leads Indian campaign, 152–57.

Cooper County (Mo.), home of Jesse B. Turley, xxvi.

Copper mines, Robert McKnight operates, 8, 20–21; trappers visit, 20–21; route via, 148.

Costilla, Indians raid, 162.

Cotton, ——, in fight with Blackfeet, 51.

Craig, William, builds Fort Davy Crockett, 54.

Crane, Delaware Indian, slain, 97.

Crow Indians, hostilities with trappers, 24–28; as neighbors, 48.

Cyane, naval vessel, 107.

DALLES of Columbia River, Frémont's party visits, 77.

177

Index

Index

Fontaine-qui-boulle (Soda Springs), Frémont visits, 74.

Fontenelle, Lucien, career, 47–48.

Fort Davy Crockett (Crockett), established, 54; described, 55.

Fort Hall, history, 46; Carson visits, 46–47, 59, 75; Lansford W. Hastings at, 90.

Fort Hempstead, in War of 1812, 3–4.

Fort Kearny, route via, 125.

Fort Laramie, suicide of Lucien Fontenelle at, 48; history, 49; Frémont visits, 67; trail to Bent's Fort, 75; Carson leaves, 68; visits, 138, 147.

Fort Leavenworth, route via, 120, 125.

Fort Massachusetts, army visits, 158, 164–65.

Fort Nez Percé, see Fort Walla Walla.

Fort Pierre, Indian agency at, 42.

Fort Robidoux (Winty, Uinta), history, 35–36. See also Brown's Hole.

Fort St. Vrain (George), history, 74–75.

Fort Union, smallpox epidemic at, 48.

Fort Vancouver, Frémont visits, 77.

Fort Walla Walla (Nez Percé), history, 45–46.

Fort William, see Bent's Fort.

Fourth of July, celebration at Bent's Fort, 87.

Fox, ——, plot to murder traders, 139–41.

Franklin (Old Franklin), home of Carsons, x, 3; scene of Carson's apprenticeship, 4.

Frederick, ——, abandons trapping, 63.

Frémont, John C., advertises Carson, xii; crosses South Park, 30; employs Antoine Godey, 45; Richard Owens, 55; Bill Williams, 63; Carson, 65–66; exploring expeditions of, 66–68, 73–119; aids Mexicans, 83; praises Carson-Godey exploit, 84–85; crosses desert, 89–91; hostilities with Gen. Castro, 93–94, 105–106; Klamath Lake detour, 95–104; campaign against Los Angeles, 107–108, 118; Carson's tribute to, 126–27.

Frémont Island, see Disappointment Island.

179

Index

GALE, Joseph, leads trappers, 59; joins Bridger, 61.

Gaunt, Capt. ———, leads trappers, 23–32.

Gila River, trappers visit, 9–10, 19–20; Indians attack Carson, 119; route via, 148.

Gillespie, Lieut. Archibald, carries message to Frémont, 96, 99; life saved, 97–98; receives Indian trophy, 104.

Godey, Antoine (Alexander), career, 45; aids Mexicans, 82–85; fights Indian, 103–104; carries Kearny's rescue appeal, 115.

Gold, reports of, 63; news of discovery, 123; deposits enrich Frémont, 126–27.

Goodel, Tim, as companion of Carson, 138.

Goose Creek, trappers visit, 59.

Grand River, Carson crosses, xxix–xxx, 123–24; route via, 88.

Grant, Blanche C., publishes Carson narrative, xvi–xvii, 5; cited xx.

Grant, Richard ("Captain Johnny"), commands Fort Hall, 46.

Grant County (N. Mex.), copper mines of, 8, 20.

Gray, Wm. H., missionary activities, 53.

Great Basin, mentioned, 13; Frémont explores, 78, 89–91.

Great Salt Lake, Frémont visits, 75–77, 89.

Green River, trappers visit, 22–23, 35, 39, 42, 52, 59; Fort Davy Crockett on, 55; Brown's Hole on, 62; route via, 87–88.

Greenhorn River, route via, 138.

Grier, Major Wm. N., leads rescue party, 131–35; career, 133; pursues Indians, 139; rescues Carson, 144–46.

Grinnell, Geo. B., article cited, 28.

Grizzly bears, Carson encounters, 38.

HAFEN, Dr. Le Roy R., aid acknowledged, xxxii; historian of Fort Laramie, 49; article cited, 55, 75.

Hammond, Lieut. Thomas C., in battle of San Pasqual, 110–13.

Index

Harvey, Alexander, daughter marries William Bent, 34.

Hastings, Lansford W., crosses desert, 90.

Hastings Cut-off, route across desert pioneered, 90.

Hernandez, Pablo, career, 85.

Higgins, James, shoots colleague, 18–19.

Holbrook, Leigh, leads pursuit of Indians, 136–37.

Horses, stolen, 20, 24, 31, 36, 40–42, 47, 64, 83, 136–37; eaten, 12–13, 20, 46, 84, 92; eat bark, 24, 49, 58; Carson procures, 109; sells, 138; rôle in battle of San Pasqual, 112–13.

Horse Creek, trappers rendezvous, 47, 59.

Houck, Louis, history cited, 4.

Howard County (Mo.) home of Carsons, 3–5.

Howitzer, abandoned, 80.

Hudson's Bay Company, expedition to California, 14; Carson joins outfit, 45; operates Fort Hall, 46.

Huerfano River, route via, 129; army visits, 158–59.

INDEPENDENCE (Mo.), ride of Aubrey from Santa Fé, 131.

Indians, warfare with whites, xxx–xxxi, ii, 3–4, 9–10, 15–17, 19–20, 24–28, 30–33, 39–42, 50–52, 56–58, 60–61, 64–65, 72–73, 82–86, 92, 95–104, 119, 121, 124, 127–29, 136–37, 139, 142–46; steal horses, 20, 24–31, 36, 40–42, 47, 64, 83, 136–37; Wm. Bent marries, 34; Carson marries, 68; smallpox ravages, 48–49, 162; sell horses, 109. See also the several tribes.

India rubber boat, Frémont uses, 76–77.

Irving, Washington, publishes Capt. Bonneville's map, 78.

JACKSON County (Col.), site of New Park, 23.

Jackson's Hole, trappers visit, 22.

Jaramillo, Francesco, father of Carson's wife, 68.

Jaramillo, Josepha, marries Carson, 34, 68–69.

Jaramillo, Maria Ignacia, wife of Charles Bent, 34.

Jicarilla Apache, see Apache Indians.

Joaquin, bandit, identified, 85.

Index

Index

Index

Muloney, Lieutenant ——, leader in Indian fight, 121.

Musselshell River, trappers visit, 48.

NAVAJO Indians, trappers visit, 9, 54.

New, William (Bill), abandons trapping, 63; Indians rob, 64; kill, 137–38.

Newberry Library, owner of Carson autobiography, xvi,xxxii; of Carson certificate, xx–xxi.

Newby, Colonel ——, aids Carson, 124–25.

New Park, identified, 23; trappers visit, 23, 62; route via, 87; Carson visits, 146.

New York City, home of Clinton Peters, xv; of Dr. De Witt C. Peters, xviii,xxi,xiii,xxv.

Norris, ——, purchases sheep, 147.

North Fork of Missouri River, see Missouri River.

North Fork of Platte River, see Platte River.

North West Company, union with Hudson's Bay Company, 14.

Northwest Fur Company, Carson joins outfit, 59.

OGDEN, Peter Skene, career, 14.

Old Franklin, see Franklin.

Old Park, trappers visit, 33; route via, 87; Carson visits, 146.

Oregon, connection of Ewing Young with, 7–8.

Oregon Trail, Fort Hall a station on, 46; first women travelers, 53; Fort Bridger on, 55; as route to Oregon, 67; emigration over, 75, 138.

Otter River, trappers visit, 48.

Owens, Richard (Dick), characterized, 55; wounded, 60; as companion of Carson, 71; establishes farm, 87–88; in Klamath Lake battle, 96, 101–102.

PARIS, home of Wm. T. Peters, xiv–xv.

Park County (Col.), site of New Park, 30.

Parker, Rev. Samuel, describes Carson-Shunar duel, 44.

Parkman, Francis, describes Fort St. Vrain, 75.

Pattie, James O., relations with Ewing Young, 7; narrative cited, 8, 17; at San Gabriel Mission, 13.

185

Index

Index

Rayado, home of Carson at, 130, 136, 146; Indians raid, 139.

Reagan, Albert B., article cited, 36–37.

Red River, Carson reaches, 139.

Republican River, route via, 74, 125.

Rio Abajo Valley, sheep purchased, 146; route via, 148.

Rio Chama, army visits, 156.

Rio Colorado, see Colorado River.

Rio del Norte, Gen. Kearny leaves, 109; route via, 148, 164; army crosses, 152–53.

Robidoux, Antoine, career, 35–36.

Robidoux, Joseph, career, 35.

Robidoux's Fort, trappers visit, 62.

Robinson, Jack, visits Robidoux's Fort, 62.

Robinson, Rebecca, marries Lindsay Carson, 3.

Rocky Mountains, as objective of John C. Frémont, 66, myth concerning river to Pacific, 78.

Ross, Alexander, narrative cited, 46.

Ruxton, George F., narrative cited, xxviii, 30, 63.

Sabin, Edwin L., biography of Carson cited, xxix, 44, 46, 48, 50, 53, 60, 105–106, 110, 137.

Sacramento, Carson visits, 147.

Sacramento, Frémont's horse, 102.

Sacramento Valley, trappers visit, 14–15; explorers view, 79; Frémont traverses, 94–95, 102–104.

Saddler, Carson learns trade, xvii, 4–5.

St. Clair (Sinclair), ——, leads trappers, 23, 54.

St. Joseph (Mo.), origin, 35.

St. Louis, McKnight party leaves, 8; Carson visits, 65, 119, 125, 141.

St. Vrain, Ceran, career, 34; kindness of, 64; popularity, 65; sends wagon-train across plains, 69; leader in Indian campaign, 163–67.

St. Vrain, Marcellus, commands Fort St. Vrain, 74.

St. Vrain Creek, Fort St. Vrain near, 74.

St. Vrain's Fork, route via, 87.

Sagundai, Delaware Indian, in Klamath Lake fight, 102.

Index

Index

Index

Index

Index

Watson, Douglas S., article cited, 123.

Weatherhead, Samuel, Carson saves, 41.

West, trans-Mississippi narratives published, xix.

"Westerns," popularity of, xix.

White, James M., family massacred, 131–34.

White, ——, in fight with Blackfeet, 51.

White Mountains, spy company visits, 158.

White River, trappers visit, 35; route via, 88.

White-rocks (Utah), Fort Robidoux near, 35–36.

Whitman, Dr. Marcus, attends rendezvous of trappers, 53.

Wiggins, Oliver, gives information, 44.

Wilkes, Commodore Charles, explorations of, 78.

Williams, Bill, mode of speech, xxviii; career, 63.

Wind River, traders rendezvous on, 52; relationship to Big Horn, 56.

Winty River, see Uinta River.

Wislizenus, Dr. F. A., narrative cited, 54–55.

Workman, David, employer of Carson, xvi, 4.

Wyeth (Wyatt), Nathaniel J., career, 59–60.

Yellowstone River, trappers visit, 45, 48, 50, 56; fight Blackfeet, 56–57.

Young, Ewing, career, 7–8; leads trapping expedition, 9–22.

Zuni, trappers visit, 9.